Prescription Drugs

Other Books in the Current Controversies Series

Prescription Drugs

Sylvia Engdahl, Book Editor

GREENHAVEN PRESS
A part of Gale, Cengage Learning

GALE
CENGAGE Learning™

Detroit • New York • San Francisco • New Haven, Conn • Waterville, Maine • London

Christine Nasso, *Publisher*
Elizabeth Des Chenes, *Managing Editor*

© 2008 Greenhaven Press, a part of Gale, Cengage Learning

Gale and Greenhaven Press are registered trademarks used herein under license.

For more information, contact:
Greenhaven Press
27500 Drake Rd.
Farmington Hills, MI 48331-3535
Or you can visit our Internet site at gale.cengage.com

For product information and technology assistance, contact us at

Gale Customer Support, 1-800-877-4253
For permission to use material from this text or product, submit all requests online at
www.cengage.com/permissions

Further permissions questions can be emailed to permissionrequest@cengage.com

Articles in Greenhaven Press anthologies are often edited for length to meet page requirements. In addition, original titles of these works are changed to clearly present the main thesis and to explicitly indicate the author's opinion. Every effort is made to ensure that Greenhaven Press accurately reflects the original intent of the authors. Every effort has been made to trace the owners of copyrighted material.

Cover image copyright Irene Pearcey, 2008. Used under license from Shutterstock.com.

LIBRARY OF CONGRESS CATALOGING-IN-PUBLICATION DATA

Prescription drugs / Sylvia Engdahl, book editor.
 p. cm. -- (Current controversies)
Includes bibliographical references and index.
ISBN 978-0-7377-3962-6 (hardcover)
ISBN 978-0-7377-3963-3 (pbk.)
1. Drugs--Public opinion. 2. Pharmaceutical industry. 3. Pharmaceutical policy.
I. Engdahl, Sylvia.
RM301.15.P735 2008
338.4'76151--dc22
2008010058

Printed in the United States of America
1 2 3 4 5 6 7 12 11 10 09 08

Contents

No: Too Much Caution Deprives Patients of Prescription Drugs They Need

Chapter 2: Do Pharmaceutical Companies Promote Unnecessary Drugs?

Chapter 3: Do Prescription Drugs in America Cost Too Much?

Yes: American Pharmaceutical Companies Charge Too Much

Chapter 4: Are Dishonest or Illegal Prescription Drug Practices Common?

Foreword

By definition, controversies are "discussions of questions in which opposing opinions clash" (Webster's Twentieth Century Dictionary Unabridged). Few would deny that controversies are a pervasive part of the human condition and exist on virtually every level of human enterprise. Controversies transpire between individuals and among groups, within nations and between nations. Controversies supply the grist necessary for progress by providing challenges and challengers to the status quo. They also create atmospheres where strife and warfare can flourish. A world without controversies would be a peaceful world; but it also would be, by and large, static and prosaic.

The Series' Purpose

The purpose of the *Current Controversies* series is to explore many of the social, political, and economic controversies dominating the national and international scenes today. Titles selected for inclusion in the series are highly focused and specific. For example, from the larger category of criminal justice, *Current Controversies* deals with specific topics such as police brutality, gun control, white collar crime, and others. The debates in *Current Controversies* also are presented in a useful, timeless fashion. Articles and book excerpts included in each title are selected if they contribute valuable, long-range ideas to the overall debate. And wherever possible, current information is enhanced with historical documents and other relevant materials. Thus, while individual titles are current in focus, every effort is made to ensure that they will not become quickly outdated. Books in the *Current Controversies* series will remain important resources for librarians, teachers, and students for many years.

In addition to keeping the titles focused and specific, great care is taken in the editorial format of each book in the series. Book introductions and chapter prefaces are offered to provide background material for readers. Chapters are organized around several key questions that are answered with diverse opinions representing all points on the political spectrum. Materials in each chapter include opinions in which authors clearly disagree as well as alternative opinions in which authors may agree on a broader issue but disagree on the possible solutions. In this way, the content of each volume in *Current Controversies* mirrors the mosaic of opinions encountered in society. Readers will quickly realize that there are many viable answers to these complex issues. By questioning each author's conclusions, students and casual readers can begin to develop the critical thinking skills so important to evaluating opinionated material.

Current Controversies is also ideal for controlled research. Each anthology in the series is composed of primary sources taken from a wide gamut of informational categories including periodicals, newspapers, books, U.S. and foreign government documents, and the publications of private and public organizations. Readers will find factual support for reports, debates, and research papers covering all areas of important issues. In addition, an annotated table of contents, an index, a book and periodical bibliography, and a list of organizations to contact are included in each book to expedite further research.

Perhaps more than ever before in history, people are confronted with diverse and contradictory information. During the Persian Gulf War, for example, the public was not only treated to minute-to-minute coverage of the war, it was also inundated with critiques of the coverage and countless analyses of the factors motivating U.S. involvement. Being able to sort through the plethora of opinions accompanying today's major issues, and to draw one's own conclusions, can be a complicated and frustrating struggle. It is the editors' hope that *Current Controversies* will help readers with this struggle.

Introduction

In recent years there has been a great deal of criticism of pharmaceutical companies. Many people believe that the cost of prescription drugs is much too high, and indeed, paying for medications is a real hardship not only for those with low incomes, but for everyone who is not wealthy—especially the elderly. Prescription drug costs have increased tremendously in the past few decades. Drug companies point out, however, that this is due to the fact that there are now a lot more drugs available for previously untreatable medical problems, and that these drugs are extremely expensive to develop. While it is true that many drugs can be manufactured cheaply, drug prices are not based on just the cost of production; they have to cover the large sums spent on research and testing.

It does not seem fair that people who are ill should have to pay more than they can afford for medication, and yet drug companies cannot be expected to sell their products at a loss.

Another issue with prescription drugs is the frequent prescribing of medications to people who are not ill in the hope of preventing future illness. Whether this practice really does prevent illness is debatable. Moreover, society's perception of "illness" has been expanding. Serious illnesses affect comparatively few people, and the cost of developing drugs for these illnesses far exceeds what could be recovered by selling them, even at high prices. Drug companies can make money only from drugs prescribed to large numbers of people. To increase their revenues, drug manufacturers vigorously promote new drugs that some observers believe are not needed, either because older, cheaper treatments for the same disease already exist or because the conditions they are designed to treat are not really diseases at all.

Two kinds of promotion are causing considerable concern at present. First, drug companies have a great deal of direct influence on doctors. As an article in the January 2008 issue of the *AARP Bulletin* states:

> For years, pharmaceutical companies have courted America's doctors with an ever-growing intensity, showering them with billions of dollars' worth of gifts, consulting fees, and trips to persuade them to prescribe their drugs. But now, patient advocates and lawmakers are out to break up those relationships, arguing that physicians—working amid the clutter of the drug industry's free samples, pens, clipboards, calculators and pizza boxes—often lose sight of the patient's best interests.

Second, drug companies advertise on television and in magazines, a practice some consumer advocates feel should be illegal. Defenders of the practice, however, believe that banning such ads would be a violation of free speech. These ads are directed not to people who are being treated for a recognized illness, but to members of the general public who have not previously believed that their problems required medication. The drug companies view such ads as educational. An increasing number of commentators view them as attempts to convince healthy people that they are sick.

A more subtle but even greater way in which the pharmaceutical industry influences the public is through information provided to the media. Most reporters are not medical experts. They do not intentionally slant what they write, but they know what makes a good story; glowing accounts of the potential benefits of a new treatment attract more readers than disclaimers about side effects, risks, or lack of evidence. If a drug company's news release omits the latter, it is likely to be taken at face value. People want to believe in the existence of cures. So do doctors, most of whom are motivated by a genuine desire to help those who consult them. It is not surprising that the idea of a "miracle drug" for every problem has taken hold.

Of course, there are many drugs that do effectively treat illness, and there is real hope that presently incurable diseases can be conquered in the future. But there is a darker side to the glorification of prescription drugs in the public mind. More and more, society is absorbing the view that the solution to all discomfort is chemical. Many industry observers assert that the drug companies have succeeded in defining some normal conditions as "diseases." In addition, they comment, young people have come to believe that every form of distress can and should be overcome by taking drugs. This is an understandable mindset for those who, since childhood, have been medicated whenever they were sick or merely unhappy, sometimes even at the insistence of school authorities. An extension of this attitude is the tendency to turn to illegally obtained drugs—both recreational and prescription—in the hope of feeling better.

Thus, prescription drug abuse is on the rise. The belief that medicines are less dangerous than banned drugs such as crack and heroin is a common, though false, belief. People who take prescription drugs without having been diagnosed with the condition the drugs were intended to treat are as likely to be harmed—or perhaps even killed—as those who take street drugs.

Until recently, it was generally assumed that medications were an unquestionable blessing. In fact, before 1938 there was no such thing as a "prescription drug"; only narcotics required a physician's authorization and prescriptions were written simply as advice. In the seventy years since controls were first established, more and more drug-related problems have arisen. Like other technologies, pharmaceuticals have brought trouble as well as benefits. Prescription drugs can be of great help to many who need them, but they should always be taken with caution.

The issues relating to prescription drugs and the pharmaceutical industry in the twenty-first century are complex and varied. The authors featured in *Current Controversies: Prescription Drugs* discuss many of these issues, from the safety and effectiveness of prescription drugs, to the promotion and marketing of new products, to the cost of prescription medications. The authors also address issues of ethics and legality, including the ways that prescription drugs are misused and abused.

Is Too Little Attention Given to the Safety Of Prescription Drugs?

Chapter Preface

Most people assume that drugs approved by the government are guaranteed to be both safe and effective—that they cause serious harm only if there has been negligence on the part of the Food and Drug Administration (FDA). But it is not as simple as that, for when it comes to drugs, "safe" is a relative term.

There is no such thing as a drug that is 100 percent safe for everyone. All drugs have multiple effects; calling the undesired ones "side" effects does not mean that they are always minor. And the action of a given drug is different on different people. So the testing of drugs is a matter of evaluating statistics, not of proving that the drug will never affect anybody adversely.

A great deal depends on how the statistics are obtained—the number of people on which the drug is tested, what other drug or placebo it is compared with, and so forth. If the test is not well designed, its results will not be valid, and medical researchers do sometimes fail to consider all the factors that should be allowed for in the design of their experiments. But even the best-designed tests cannot uncover all the adverse effects a drug may have, because these effects may not occur until the drug has been taken by millions of patients. Or they may not show up until it has been used for a longer period of time than any test can last.

So whether a drug should be called safe is not an absolute judgment, and there is controversy about where to draw the line. For instance, how long should testing continue? If the drug is put on the market too quickly, adverse effects—perhaps even fatal ones—may later appear. On the other hand, if its approval is delayed too long, people who could be helped by it may suffer unnecessarily and, in some cases, may die while they are waiting.

Is it worse for a few people to be harmed by a new drug than for many others to be harmed by the lack of it? The answer to this question depends in part on the number of people likely to be affected, but that number cannot be known in advance. Furthermore, few would say that it is acceptable for a drug to do serious damage to some patients, even if far more will be helped by its availability. If damaging effects are known to be rare, some researchers believe that the benefits to the public justify approval of the drug. Another question must be asked, however: How serious are those effects, especially when compared to the condition the drug is intended to treat?

It would seem obvious that minor health problems do not warrant the use of dangerous drugs. But not everyone agrees about what problems are minor. For example, many widely promoted drugs, such as those that lower cholesterol, are designed not to cure illness, but to lessen the *statistical* chance of future illness—in other words, to reduce "risk factors," which in themselves have recently been defined as "disease." The individuals who take such drugs might never develop the illnesses they are trying to avoid. Is the attempt at prevention worth the risk of harmful side effects, especially considering that only some who take such drugs would have later been affected by the disease? That issue is rarely raised; fear that serious illness will strike in the future distracts both doctors and patients from asking whether preventative medication might do more harm than good.

Off-Label Prescription of Drugs Can Lead to Adverse Effects

Hazel Muir

Hazel Muir writes for the British magazine New Scientist.

It seems like a foregone conclusion. People with mild symptoms of irregular heartbeat have a higher risk of sudden death. So give them drugs proven to help treat arrhythmia and you'll save lives.

This was just what doctors did in the 1980s. There was one problem: the drugs had been tested on and approved for people with severe arrhythmias. When clinical trials were eventually carried out in people with mild arrhythmias, they showed that, contrary to all expectations, the drugs doubled or tripled the risk of death.

"We were just shocked by what we saw," says pharmacologist Raymond Woosley, now at the University of Arizona in Tucson, whose team did the trials. "It took a long time for people to stop prescribing these drugs because they just couldn't believe it." It was later concluded that the heart drugs had killed 50,000 people. "That is a huge number. It was amazing to me that there wasn't more hue and cry."

Doctors do not have to tell you that your prescription is off-label, and no one bothers to track who benefits and who suffers.

Many Drugs Prescribed "Off-Label"

This is an example of what can happen when drugs are prescribed "off-label," meaning that they are used in a way not approved by regulators. Two decades on from the heart-drug scandal, you might think that it would be impossible for the same thing to happen again. Far from it. A report published [in early 2006] concluded that a fifth of prescriptions in the US are for drugs that have not been approved for the condition from which the patient is suffering. More importantly, for three-quarters of these prescriptions there is little if any scientific rationale. "What we've found over and over is that you cannot just assume the benefit will be there," says Woosley.

Prescribing drugs off-label is sometimes described as a form of human experimentation. But while a proper medical experiment involves volunteers and careful recording of results, doctors do not have to tell you that your prescription is off-label, and no one bothers to track who benefits and who suffers. Drugs can be used in non-approved ways for many years without anyone checking the outcomes.

This means people are probably still being killed by off-label prescriptions. "I can almost guarantee it," Woosley says. "All drugs can cause harm." So why do doctors persist in using drugs in ways for which there is little or no evidence? And what can be done about it?

The agencies that regulate drugs, such as the US Food and Drug Administration (FDA) or the UK's Medicines and Healthcare Products Regulatory Agency, demand that drug companies conduct rigorous clinical trials to prove a drug's safety and effectiveness in treating a particular disease. Then they approve the drug and its label, describing how the drug should be given, to whom and at what dosage. But these guidelines are not binding. Doctors can, with a few exceptions, prescribe drugs any way they want.

In many cases they have little choice. The most common form of off-label usage is to give drugs to people in groups on which it has not been tested, such as pregnant women, babies and children. Drug companies are naturally reluctant to run trials involving such people. Surveys of children's wards in hospitals across Europe suggest that nearly half of all drug prescriptions are off-label.

Depriving Patients

With this kind of off-label prescription, there is usually little doubt that a drug will help treat the condition for which it is given: the main issues are safety and dosage. Things become less clear, though, when a drug approved for one condition is used to treat another. This form of off-label prescribing is a natural last resort when seriously ill patients do not respond to standard treatments, or for rare diseases for which there is no approved treatment at all.

In countries where doctors will not use a drug until it gets the green light from a regulator like the FDA, many people who desperately need a drug do not get it.

Yet off-label usage is not restricted to these extreme situations. Non-approved drugs are used to treat many common conditions for which approved treatments are available. Doctors argue this is justified because the pace of medical discovery is faster than the regulatory machinery: if an off-label treatment is the best option, surely it would be wrong to deprive patients of it just because the regulator hasn't rubber-stamped it yet?

"We have a policy, and it's enshrined in US law, that we don't want to let the government dictate to doctors how they should practise medicine," says Maxwell Mehlman, an expert on medical law at Case Western Reserve University in Cleveland, Ohio. "The FDA can say whether a drug is safe or effective, but it can't tell doctors what to use it for."

Indeed, in countries where doctors will not use a drug until it gets the green light from a regulator like the FDA, many people who desperately need a drug do not get it. Andrew

Weeks, an obstetrician at the University of Liverpool, UK, highlights the case of misoprostol, a type of prostaglandin. When the FDA approved misoprostol to prevent stomach ulcers in 1988, obstetricians were intrigued, as prostaglandins are usually used to induce labour in pregnant women and prevent haemorrhage after birth. "In the Third World, the biggest maternal killer is haemorrhage following delivery," says Weeks.

Unlike other prostaglandins, misoprostol is very cheap, can be taken orally and does not need to be kept in a fridge. It seemed the ideal drug for women in developing countries. But misoprostol was a political hot potato in the US, because it can be used for abortion. Searle, the company that introduced the drug, did not want FDA approval for reproductive uses, so this research had to be publicly funded and was grindingly slow. The safe doses for inducing labour have only recently been established. Yet if doctors around the world did not use misoprostol off-label, many women would suffer as a result.

Scientific Basis Is Lacking

So there are good reasons for off-label prescriptions. Yet until a drug has been approved for a particular group of people or for treating a particular condition, how do doctors know whether it works, whether it is safe and what dosage to use? How do they know if it will turn out to save lives like misoprostol or harm them like the arrhythmia drugs? The answer is that in most cases they don't. The scientific basis for many off-label treatments is flaky at best, says Randall Stafford, an epidemiologist at Stanford University in California.

In May [2006] he and his colleagues published their analysis of data from the National Disease and Therapeutic Index, an ongoing survey of office-based doctors in the US. In 2001, the survey sampled over 400,000 prescriptions given to patients. Stafford's team looked at patterns of prescribing for the 100 most commonly used drugs, as well as 60 others randomly chosen. They found that a fifth of prescriptions were for a condition for which the drugs were not approved by the FDA.

Then the team looked at whether these off-label uses had scientific support, in the sense of having been proven to be effective in controlled clinical trials or at least fairly large observational studies. The team found that three-quarters of the off-label prescriptions had little or no scientific support.

Top of the list was gabapentin (Neurontin), approved by the FDA for the treatment of epileptic seizures and pain from shingles. Yet 83 per cent of gabapentin prescriptions were for other conditions. For some of these off-label uses, such as easing social phobia and preventing migraines, there was scientific support. But two-thirds of all gabapentin prescriptions were for diseases that it might not be effective for, including bipolar disorder, depression and back pain. . . .

Illegal Marketing

So why do doctors prescribe drugs off-label without good cause? Often, it just seems logical. It made sense that misoprostol would have similar effects to other prostaglandins, and this proved to be the case. But it also made sense that arrhythmia drugs would help in mild cases, and that turned out to be disastrously wrong.

Patients and doctors alike . . . try out new drugs on the grounds that "newer is better.". . . Newer is not necessarily better, but it is usually more expensive.

The kind of "function creep" seen in the case of the arrhythmia drugs is common. Doctors tend to assume that if a drug works for one form of a condition, it will work for another. Almost all clinical trials of drugs for treating manic depression, for instance, have involved patients with the most severe form of the disease, called bipolar I. Now many such drugs are being dished out to people with milder forms.

Stafford says there is also a tendency among patients and doctors alike to try out new drugs on the grounds that "newer is better." This is troublesome, he says, because newer is not necessarily better, but it is usually more expensive. Sometimes doctors might be persuaded of a drug's usefulness by early results presented at conferences, which may or may not be confirmed by later trials. And sometimes they are persuaded by the marketing tactics of drug companies.

The FDA forbids companies promoting off-label uses of drugs directly to patients, but they can promote such uses to doctors with certain provisos. The companies sometimes break the rules, though. In 2004, drug giant Pfizer pleaded guilty to criminal charges because its Warner-Lambert division illegally promoted gabapentin for a host of off-label conditions. Company sales reps had paid doctors to give talks about off-label uses of gabapentin and to put their names to ghost-written articles singing its praises. The doctors received generous "consulting" fees as well as expenses-paid jollies to the 1996 summer Olympics. Pfizer was eventually forced to pay $430 million in penalties. "That is the most dramatic case that I'm aware of, but there have been a few others," says Mehlman.

In Stafford's study, gabapentin turned out to have the highest off-label prescription rate for any single drug. There is no proof that the illegal marketing was behind that, but Stafford says it certainly suggests that the influence of illegal off-label marketing deserves further investigation.

Death of the Industry

So what should be done to prevent a repetition of the arrhythmia scandal? Everyone agrees that simply stopping off-label prescribing is not the answer. "If we were to ban unapproved uses, or restrict them to very formal research contexts, lots of people would not get treatments they need," says Mehlman.

Weeks thinks clear guidance from agencies like the UK National Institute for Health and Clinical Excellence (NICE) is the key. NICE's role is to make recommendations based on reviews of all the existing evidence. "If NICE recommends how to use a drug, everyone uses it and nobody actually cares whether it's off-label," he says.

Mehlman and Stafford would like to see an automated warning system that would be triggered when a doctor logs an off-label prescription. The system could suggest approved alternatives, and if the doctor persisted with their initial prescription it could store information about their reasons for doing so. That would both reduce off-label prescriptions and also create a clearer picture of off-label usage. . . .

Mehlman argues for more radical measures as well. He thinks that if a company earns large profits from the sale of a drug for an off-label use, it should be forced to do trials on that use and seek FDA approval if it wants to continue selling the drug. "If manufacturers had more obligations to monitor and test off-label uses, then in return they might be able to talk about them more," says Mehlman. "That would be a fair trade-off."

Woosley disagrees, saying the expense would drive companies out of business. "I think that would be the death of the industry," he says. He argues instead that there should be more government funding for research on off-label usage, and that technology should be playing a much more effective role in establishing the safety of all drugs, whether off-label or not. "It amazes me that you can get on the Internet and find out how many suitcases an airline lost this month, but you cannot find out how many people were harmed by a medication," says Woosley. He thinks doctors should record poor drug outcomes in a national computer network that would flag up common problems.

Everyone agrees that vigorous improvements in surveillance of drug prescriptions, and of what happens to the patients who receive them, are essential to drag drug prescribing towards a more evidence-based footing. The current progress is inadequate, Stafford says. Over the coming year he plans to calculate the financial cost of all the new drugs prescribed off-label in the US to people who might not benefit from them at all. Perhaps that mountain of dollars will finally spur some action.

Some Prescription Drugs on the Market Are Unsafe

Consumer Reports

Consumer Reports *is published by Consumers Union, an independent nonprofit organization with the goals of informing and protecting consumers and working toward a fair and safe marketplace.*

U.S. consumers have been buffeted by bad news about the safety of the prescription drugs they take. One shock was the revelation of serious heart risks from the pain reliever Vioxx. Then "black box" warnings [a warning that appears on package inserts for prescription drugs, named for the black border surrounding the text] about an increased risk of suicide in young people were slapped on all antidepressants.

A leader of the Food and Drug Administration's [FDA's] drug-safety office has told Congress that the agency and its once-vaunted Center for Drug Evaluation and Research are "broken." The FDA is currently the object of several investigations, including one initiated at its own request.

A *Consumer Reports* investigation has now found that tens of millions of people may unknowingly have been exposed to the rare but serious side effects of a dozen relatively common prescription drug types. Collectively, the drugs, sold in 140 brand-name or generic versions, accounted for some 266 million prescriptions in the U.S. and almost $25 billion in sales during the 12 months ending in September 2005, according to NDCHealth, an Atlanta-based health-care-information company.

Almost all of the drugs are used to treat relatively common conditions that are not usually crippling or life-

Consumer Reports, "Prescription for Trouble," January 2006, pp. 34–38. Copyright © 2006 Consumers Union of the U.S. Inc., Yonkers, NY 10703-1057, www.ConsumerReports.org, a nonprofit organization. Reprinted with permission for educational purposes only. No commercial use or reproduction permitted.

threatening, such as acne, eczema and head lice. None is the only drug option. Among the 12, which are made by a wide range of manufacturers, are the pain reliever celecoxib (Celebrex), a close cousin of Vioxx, linked with heart attack and stroke; the cholesterol reducer rosuvastatin (Crestor), which may cause muscle breakdown and kidney damage; and the eczema drugs pimecrolimus (Elidel) and tacrolimus (Protopic), which may increase the risk of cancer.

The 12 drug types we have identified are not a "dirty dozen." There are plenty of others with worse risks, such as those used to treat cancer or severe rheumatoid arthritis. And each of the 12 types has legitimate medical uses, especially when other treatments fail.

Even a perfect drug-safety system might miss some of the adverse effects of medicines before they hit the market.

But their known or possible adverse effects—which include heart attack, stroke, kidney failure, irreversible bone loss, and cancer—were undetected or underestimated when the FDA approved them for use. Some still don't carry a black-box warning—the most serious label alert—that our chief medical adviser says they should.

Even a perfect drug-safety system might miss some of the adverse effects of medicines before they hit the market. But our investigation has identified serious flaws in both the initial drug-approval process and the monitoring of products after they reach the market, which have almost surely delayed the detection and public disclosure of adverse reactions of many widely sold medications. Indeed, our investigation suggests that our list of 12 is not exhaustive.

An Absence of Leadership

The problem with the drug-safety system starts with the FDA. The agency's regulatory might has been undercut by constraints on its enforcement power, limited resources, dependency on drug-company fees to help finance the approval process, and what critics claim is a lack of will to enforce tough requirements.

Drug companies have often failed to conduct the studies needed to identify risks that often emerge after approval.

In a statement by e-mail, Susan Cruzan, an FDA spokeswoman, said, "Drug safety has been and will continue to be a top priority for us." Cruzan added that "a recent internal audit showed that our professional staff spends about one-half its time addressing safety issues." . . .

Compounding the safety problem drug companies have often failed to conduct the studies needed to identify risks that often emerge after approval. Wide distribution of newly approved drugs before their long-term safety has been established, plus immediate, heavy, and sometimes misleading advertising, may increase the chance of harm.

Consumer Reports' exclusive, ongoing analysis of consumer-drug ads identified a wide range of inaccurate information about safety and efficacy, including what the FDA deemed misleading claims for some brands of every high-risk drug we identified, except the malaria and head-lice medications. Our analysis further suggests that the FDA's regulation of drug ads has weakened considerably since the late 1990s, although we found some improvement in the past two years [2004–2005.]

Some companies have withheld publication of studies that found serious risks, or have failed to conduct post-approval studies that they promised to the FDA. Such studies are crucial for promptly detecting adverse reactions that surface when large numbers of consumers start to use new medications.

The safety system's failings were illustrated in October 2005. A study released first on the Web site of the *Journal of the American Medical Association (JAMA)* reported that the diabetes drug muraglitazar, which an FDA advisory committee had recommended approving six weeks earlier, appeared to double the risk of heart attack, stroke, or death. Some analysts expected the drug to be a billion-dollar seller, but now drug-maker Bristol-Myers Squibb says it's talking with Merck, its cosponsor, about scrapping the application or conducting more studies.

That report averted "a potential catastrophe," says Steven Nissen, M.D., medical director of the Cleveland Cardiovascular Coordinating Center. Nissen, lead researcher of the *JAMA* study, said in a phone interview that "the advisory panel just dropped the ball completely."

An accompanying editorial in *JAMA* reported that the study results were presented to the FDA in ways that may have fostered an "illusion of safety." Tony Plohoros, a Bristol-Myers Squibb spokesman, said by e-mail that the company's analytic methods "are widely used and have been validated by the scientific community." The FDA would not offer specific comments while a decision on the drug was pending.

FDA: From Watchdog to Lapdog?

Once touted the world's most rigorous drug regulator, the FDA is now being scrutinized by congressional committees and the Government Accountability Office for possible regulatory lapses.

The agency's transformation started in the 1980s, when AIDS and cancer activists pushed for quicker access to potentially life-prolonging drugs for severely ill patients. But that acceleration was subsequently applied to all medicines, including those for problems that aren't life-threatening as well as for "me too" drugs, which offer little or no advantage over existing medicines whose risks are well known.

In 1992 Congress passed the Prescription Drug User Fee Act (PDUFA), which forced a sea change at the FDA. The law imposed tight deadlines for drug evaluation and required companies to pay fees earmarked for hiring more reviewers. In fiscal year 2004 the FDA collected some $250 million from drug companies, almost half of its drug-review budget. That year, the agency boasted in a report to the president and Congress that "drug-approval time has been cut almost in half" since the advent of PDUFA.

Current deadlines require that reviews be completed within 10 months for standard drugs, compared with an average of more than 20 months before PDUFA; priority drugs, including at least two high-risk medicines on our list, Celebrex and Zelnorm, are assessed in 6 months. The FDA maintains that it hasn't lowered its standards. But even with the extra reviewers, meeting the deadlines can be difficult.

Close to 20 percent of FDA reviewers say they "have felt pressured to approve or recommend approval" of a drug.

"With the clock ticking, you did the best you could," says Elizabeth Barbehenn, Ph.D., a drug reviewer at the FDA's Office of New Drugs for 13 years before leaving in 1998 for the nonprofit Public Citizen Health Research Group. "It was extraordinarily frustrating."

Close to 20 percent of FDA reviewers say they "have felt pressured to approve or recommend approval" of a drug despite "reservations about its safety, efficacy, or quality," according to a 2003 survey of some 400 agency reviewers by the Department of Health and Human Services' inspector general. Fewer than one-fourth of the 400 indicated that the "work environment" allowed "expression of differing scientific opinions." The accompanying report concluded: "Workload pressures increasingly challenge" the effectiveness of the review process. . . .

The data with which FDA reviewers work aren't always the best. Federal law allows drugmakers to submit as few as one clinical trial plus confirmatory evidence. Typically companies need show only that their product works better than a placebo, rather than an established drug, to achieve an effect that may have little relevance for patient outcomes, according to an opinion piece in the Sept. 8, 2005, issue of the *New England Journal of Medicine*. Such a "minimal standard" would be "unacceptable anywhere else in research," the piece said.

Some of the studies, involving drugs that will be taken for decades, last as little as a few months, said Marcia Angell, M.D., former editor-in-chief of the *New England Journal of Medicine*, by e-mail. She added that drug companies typically recruit patients who are younger and healthier than those who would ultimately use the drug. Such patients "are less likely to experience side effects," Angell said. . . .

Powerless After Approval

While longer, more realistic studies and tighter scrutiny should theoretically detect more risks before approval, some hazards will unavoidably emerge only after drugs are used by a larger group of consumers. Monitoring such "postmarketing" drug reactions is therefore critical.

But the FDA lacks the legal authority to force companies to do the necessary research. In a report in the *Federal Register* in February 2005, the agency noted that companies had committed to conducting 1,191 postmarketing studies of approved drugs. But 68 percent were still "pending" as of late September 2004, meaning they hadn't been started.

Many of those studies were pending for good reasons, [associate vice president for regulatory affairs at the Pharmaceutical Research and Manufacturers of America Alan] Goldhammer says, notably difficulty lining up research sites and recruiting patients. But Randy Juhl, Ph.D., a former dean of the School of Pharmacy at the University of Pittsburgh and a former FDA advisory panel member, says the drug companies' failure to meet postmarketing study commitments shows that they "do not take these responsibilities seriously." The FDA should ask Congress "for additional enforcement power," possibly an "umpteen-million-dollar fine per day" to get the studies done, he says.

An injection of resources may be equally important: The FDA's Office of Drug Safety, which monitors adverse reactions to a medication after approval, is one-tenth the size of the agency's Office of New Drugs, which handles the original approval process. And the new-drug office, not the safety office, has the final say about post-approval safety concerns.

That's a bad setup, says Eric J. Topol, M.D., chairman of the department of cardiovascular medicine at the Cleveland Clinic and a former FDA advisory panel member. New-drug officials who approve the medication in the first place are, in effect, "champions of the drug," he said. "They cannot be objective if safety issues arise after it's marketed," he added. . . .

David Graham, M.D., associate director for science and medicine at the FDA's Office of Drug Safety, testified before a Senate committee in November 2004 that officials in the new-drug office had made clear that his department should not offer recommendations that contradict their department. He said, too, that senior management in his own office pressured him to change his conclusion that high doses of the pain reliever Vioxx increased the risk of heart attack.

The FDA immediately issued a denial, stating that Graham's testimony "does not reflect the views of the agency." Drug-safety scientists have "independent authority," and "when drug safety issues are identified, they must be factored into the risk-benefit equation," the statement said.

Weakness About Warnings

The FDA cannot force companies to add newly emergent risks to drug labels. "I think it's unconscionable," says Arthur Levin, M.P.H., director of the Center for Medical Consumers in New York City, a nonprofit advocacy organization. "We want the FDA to get stricter about this stuff, but we don't give them the means to enforce their decisions."

Six of the 12 high-risk drug types we identified had no black-box warning, the strongest kind, when we went to press [at the end of 2005], though in most of those cases the FDA should request that warning, says Marvin Lipman, M.D., chief medical advisor for Consumers Union, the publisher of *Consumer Reports*. . . .

Misleading Drug Ads

The FDA further weakened the drug-safety system when it relaxed restrictions on direct-to-consumer drug ads in 1997 and opened the floodgates to broadcast ads of newly approved drugs, whose risks may not yet be known.

Consumer Reports' analysis of regulatory letters that the FDA posted on its Web site from January 1997 through September 2005 reveals that consumer-drug ads have contained a wide range of misleading messages: minimizing the risks, exaggerating the efficacy, misstating or omitting the labeling information, making false superiority claims, and promoting unapproved uses for an approved drug.

Our analysis suggests that the FDA has tried to get stricter with advertisers. Starting in 2004, it sent manufacturers significantly more warning letters, which may order drugmakers to run remedial ads or send corrective letters to doctors.

Companies have sometimes reported only the positive findings of drug studies and suppressed the disappointing or worrisome ones.

But the number of less serious "notice of violation" letters dropped sharply, starting in 1999, and has stayed low. . . .

Hidden Risks

It's not just the advertising that may be misleading. Companies have sometimes reported only the positive findings of drug studies and suppressed the disappointing or worrisome ones. That "has a huge distorting effect on what we know about drugs," says Nissen, lead author of the muraglitazar study.

In April 2002 GlaxoSmithKline submitted three studies to the FDA to support an application for approval of children's use of its antidepressant Paxil. Two studies failed to show that the drug was effective against depression; the combined results of the three studies suggested an increased risk of suicidal thinking and behavior. But the company published only the single positive study, in the July 2001 issue of the *Journal of the American Academy of Child and Adolescent Psychiatry*.

In June 2003, about a year after receiving the studies about increased risk, the FDA issued a statement on its Web site saying that although it had "not completed its evaluation of the new safety data," it was recommending against prescribing Paxil for children and adolescents. Another 16 months passed before the FDA requested a strong suicide-warning label for Paxil and all other antidepressants.

Mary Anne Rhyne, a spokeswoman for GlaxoSmithKline, says the FDA-requested label changes were "implemented immediately." But by that time, although Paxil was never approved for pediatric use, doctors had written an estimated 2.1 million "off label," or unapproved-use, prescriptions for children.

A lawsuit filed by New York's attorney general in June 2004 charged the drug giant with concealing information about Paxil and misrepresenting the research to its own sales representatives, telling them that the drug had "remarkable efficacy and safety in the treatment of adolescent depression." GlaxoSmithKline admitted no wrongdoing but resolved the lawsuit by agreeing to pay New York $2.5 million "to avoid protracted litigation."

Rhyne confirmed that the company faces similar lawsuits from Paxil users as well as suits claiming attempted or actual suicide. . . .

To end selective reporting, legislation known as the Fair Access to Clinical Trials Act has been introduced in Congress [and is still in committee as of March 2008] to require registration of virtually all pending clinical drug trials on a government-run public Web site. It would also mandate posting the results on a database accessible to doctors and patients. The American Medical Association has recommended that the Department of Health and Human Services establish a comprehensive drug-trials registry. And the editors of 13 top medical journals have agreed to publish only trials listed on an acceptable registry. . . .

Doctors Fail to Report

Physicians are supposed to voluntarily report any serious drug reactions to the FDA's MedWatch program, where researchers look for signals that a medication might be causing problems. But only 1 to 10 percent of such incidents are ever reported, various studies have estimated. An FDA analysis found that pharmacists and, to a lesser extent, consumers each filed far more MedWatch reports than did physicians in fiscal 2004. Nurses filed about as many as doctors.

The FDA's drug-safety and risk-management advisory committee has recommended that the agency actively search databases for signs of trouble. Until now, the FDA has consistently "underinvested" in such high-tech information gathering, reported Scott Gottlieb, M.D., the FDA's deputy commissioner for medical and scientific affairs, in the July/August 2005 issue of *Health Affairs*.

The FDA has recently taken stronger action in some areas. In addition to issuing more warning letters about misleading ads, it has begun releasing information on its Web site about possible adverse drug effects even before the information has been fully vetted, according to postings on the site. And it promises to expand those early warnings on a new Drug Watch Web page. At press time, it had issued 12 public-health advisories on major drug side effects in 2005, which is more than in the past four years combined. And since October 2004, it has persuaded companies to add black-box drug warnings to all antidepressants, which are on our high-risk list, and all nonsteroidal anti-inflammatory drugs.

Prescription Drugs Can Cause Serious Harm When Risks Are Ignored

Susan Kelleher

Susan Kelleher is a reporter for the Seattle Times.

W hen Tami Melum hugs her heart-shaped pillow, she can feel the pain of the past three years seep into the surgical scar on her chest.

"It reminds me of how the kids and my husband suffered," Melum said of the pillow, which was given to her after open-heart surgery and usually sits on a bedroom dresser in her Sedro-Woolley [Washington] home. "I keep it there as a reminder."

Melum, 39, took weight-loss drugs so she could feel healthier and keep up with her two boys, now 11 and 13. The drugs nearly killed her.

After being prescribed Redux and a drug combination known as "phen-fen," Melum developed heart damage so severe that in 2002 surgeons had to cut open her chest and heart and install an artificial valve. She is a tragic testament to what can go wrong in a system where the powerful pharmaceutical industry influences what constitutes a disease, who has it, and how it should be treated.

Before taking the drugs, Melum was overweight but healthy: Her cholesterol, blood pressure and blood sugar were all normal.

But that wasn't enough. By the mid-1990s, the medical establishment had changed its mind about people such as Melum. Some of the world's most prominent obesity experts, with backing from the drug industry and medical societies, defined obesity as a stand-alone "disease" that caused premature death and needed to be treated with drugs. Suddenly, Tami Melum and millions like her were, by definition, sick.

The story of obesity shows how it became acceptable for doctors to risk killing or injuring people on the premise that it would save them from illnesses they might never get.

In making obesity a disease, these experts helped create a billion-dollar market for the drugs that maimed Melum, killed hundreds, and damaged the hearts and lungs of tens of thousands.

The story of obesity shows how it became acceptable for doctors to risk killing or injuring people on the premise that it would save them from illnesses they might never get.

Creating a "Disease"

How did the fight against fat reach this point?

It started more than a decade ago as drug companies and their scientific consultants increasingly promoted using a Body Mass Index (BMI) of 30 as the trigger point for when someone should be treated for obesity, including being prescribed weight-loss drugs. The BMI is a height-to-weight ratio that provides a rough estimate of body fat. Adapted from life-insurance company measures three decades ago, the BMI not only measures obesity but also sets ranges for "ideal weight" and "overweight.". . .

At the time the BMI standard was being promoted as a disease, only two prescription weight-loss drugs were available in the United States: phentermine, approved by the Food and Drug Administration (FDA) in 1959, and fenfluramine, sold as Pondimin, approved in 1973. In the early 1990s, doctors began prescribing them together for weight loss, and a diet craze took off. The FDA had not signed off on the safety of the two being used together. This "off-label" use of phen-fen therefore carried unknown risks for patients and their prescribing doctors.

With a new drug in the pipeline, the [drug] industry ... demonstrated a new urgency to define obesity as a chronic disease ... treated with its own drug.

With the patent on Pondimin soon to expire, a drug company formulated a blend of molecules in the two drugs and created Redux, dexfenfluramine. Like phen-fen, it gave its users the feeling of being full.

With a new drug in the pipeline, the industry and its experts demonstrated a new urgency to define obesity as a chronic disease that should be treated with its own drug.

In May 1995, the National Institutes of Health (NIH) asked 24 experts to write guidelines for diagnosing and treating obesity. The expert panel officially defined obesity as a BMI of 30 or higher, and overweight as a BMI above 25 and below 30. The panel, which included the pharmacologist who created the phen-fen combo, was criticized for its ties to the drug and weight-loss industries.

The FDA Hearings

In fall 1995, the FDA first took up the approval of Redux, owned at the time by Interneuron Pharmaceuticals. If approved, Redux would be the first new weight-loss drug in more than 20 years.

At the hearings, Interneuron presented data showing an obesity pandemic and said desperate measures were required to stop it from prematurely killing 300,000 Americans a year. That controversial figure came from weight-loss experts and researchers who used epidemiological data from decades-old health studies to build the case that excess body fat was a crisis more urgent than even AIDS. They estimated the economic cost in health care, including associated heart attacks, diabetes and other diseases, to be more than $60 billion a year.

The high costs and daunting death toll bolstered support for physicians to apply risky treatments to the obese, such as gastric bypass surgery, stomach banding or long-term courses of drugs that would be too dangerous to give to healthy people.

Although phen-fen and Redux were billed as lifesavers, they also were known to have fatal side effects in certain cases.

At the FDA hearing, Interneuron and its experts presented grisly calculations in support of Redux's approval: For every nine people who died from the drug in a given year, 280 people would be saved from premature deaths. The company's chief scientific officer, Dr. Bobby Sandage, told the FDA panel that, despite expected deaths, the drug had "a highly favorable safety profile given the morbidity and mortality of obesity." . . .

At the hearing was a newly formed group, the American Obesity Association, which built a case for treating obesity as a chronic disease. Funded largely by drug companies, including two involved with Redux, the association was headed by Dr. Richard Atkinson, an internist who advocated gastric bypass for severe obesity and who later founded a company to test for what he believed might be an "obesity virus." At the hearing, the association positioned itself as a patient-advocacy organization, though it offered no patients to testify for the drug.

When drugs are given to people on the margins of disease, the number of people harmed with little benefit increases exponentially.

Dr. Leo Lutwak, the FDA scientist who evaluated Redux, opposed its approval, saying it was too risky for what he thought were only modest weight losses. He said he was concerned about the drug's effect on the brain and its "frightening" association with pulmonary hypertension, an irreparable and often fatal lung disease.

Although few in the field questioned that obesity in its extreme form posed substantial health risks, less was known about the health risks for those who were marginally obese. When drugs are given to people on the margins of disease, the number of people harmed with little benefit increases exponentially, critics said.

The FDA committee members discussed the troubling data surrounding Redux for nine hours and voted 5-3 against its approval. After impassioned pleas from one member, the committee took a second vote, but the 3-2 vote for approval was voided because some members had left. Another meeting was scheduled for November [1995]. . . .

The committee voted 6-5 in November to recommend approval, and in April the FDA gave the drug clearance for long-term use. The drug went on sale in May 1996. Prescriptions for the drug that year topped 18 million.

Pills' High Cost

Melum, then a 30-year-old mother of two in Skagit County [Washington], was swept into the anti-fat fervor by her doctor, who shared the same health club and noticed how hard Melum was working to lose the weight she had gained during her second pregnancy. . . .

Across the country, Redux users were suffering heart damage, a side effect the drug maker never mentioned.

Melum took the phen-fen combination for six months starting in February 1996. In one month, she lost 22 pounds from her 5-foot-5-inch frame, dropping to 203. She lost another 13 pounds over the next six months. "It worked great, I have to admit," she said. She took Redux for two or three months, and when it seemed to stop working, resumed taking phen-fen for about five more months. Melum said she doesn't recall discussing the known risks with her doctor when she began taking phen-fen and Redux.

At the time, the drug maker noted what it said were rare instances of lung damage but nothing else of significance. But across the country, Redux users were suffering heart damage, a side effect the drug maker never mentioned.

The first outsider to publicly warn about Redux and heart damage was a medical technician at a Fargo, N.D., clinic. She noticed that echocardiograms of younger women, with no history of heart disease, showed severely damaged heart valves after taking the diet drugs. The doctor she worked for sent two dozen case files to the Mayo Clinic. There at the clinic, cardiologists researched the matter and concluded that Redux and phen-fen were linked to heart-valve damage. The clinic announced this startling finding in summer 1997, and the FDA followed up with its own warning about the drugs to doctors, hospitals and the public.

Unaware, Melum took the drugs until September 1997, when a local pharmacist told her they had been pulled from the market. He told her she might be able to get her prescription filled elsewhere. She tried without success but went on with her workouts.

In fact, Wyeth, which by then held the license to Redux, had pulled the drug from the market that month. It also stopped selling Pondimin, its brand-name fenfluramine, half of the phen-fen combo.

Melum said her doctor, Nadine Burrington in Mount Vernon, never contacted her after news broke of the potentially deadly side effects. Melum said the doctor eventually apologized and told her she had no idea the drugs would harm her. . . .

The first information Melum received about potential problems with her heart came in early 2001 in the form of an information packet Wyeth sent her. The mailing was part of its proposed legal settlement with hundreds of thousands of patients in a class-action lawsuit. Melum said she kept the information but ignored it until fall 2001. At a friend's urging, she applied for Wyeth's free testing, which discovered her valve damage.

"The doctor told me if I had waited much longer, I would be a candidate for [a heart] transplant," Melum said.

In May 2002, a surgeon sawed through Melum's sternum, cut into her heart and replaced a valve that controls blood flow on the left side of her heart. Within three weeks, she suffered an allergic reaction to the anesthesia and was hospitalized. Two days later, she was near death.

In emergency surgery at the University of Washington Medical Center, doctors inserted a tube in her chest and siphoned more than three quarts of fluid from her heart. Her husband, Glenn, watched and wondered how he was going to raise the boys by himself. "I was standing there watching her just slip away from me," he said in an interview, looking to the ceiling to keep tears at bay.

The medical bills related to her surgeries topped $140,000.

Wyeth established a $3.7 billion trust fund for injured patients in 2000 as part of a proposed settlement and created a $1.2 billion supplemental fund for patients [in 2005]. Wyeth said it expects to pay $21.1 billion to settle legal claims involving phen-fen and Redux.

Melum joined the lawsuit and settled her claim in December [2004]. After fees, she received $500,000. She now weighs more than when she started the drugs, has an eight-inch scar down her chest, and will have to take a daily blood thinner for life.

Ongoing Controversy

The industry lost a blockbuster obesity drug, but more were in development. In the years after the Redux fiasco, the weight-loss industry—doctors, nutritionists, weight-loss clinics, drug makers—supported efforts to keep obesity classified as a disease and successfully lobbied for insurance to cover its treatment. . . .

Recently, a study by the federal Centers for Disease Control and Prevention challenged the conventional wisdom that the nation faces a medical crisis caused by fat.

In fact, carrying a few extra pounds may prolong life, especially in the elderly, the study shows. People who are overweight, but not obese, have a lower death risk than people of normal weight, according to the study. Obese people, except for those who are extremely obese, face only a slightly increased risk of death from their weight, the study shows.

The study's federal scientists discounted previous estimates of 300,000 annual deaths due to obesity, the controversial figure used by pharmaceutical companies to justify selling the risky weight-loss drugs. Authors of the new study said the 300,000 figure had been exaggerated by selective data and faulty analysis. Instead, obesity was associated with 112,000 deaths each year—most of them in extremely obese people, the study said. Being underweight had risks, too, and was said to be responsible for 34,000 premature deaths a year. . . .

One person who will be paying close attention to the debate is Tami Melum. Had she known then what she knows now, she never would have taken the risk that the drug-company experts minimized in their battle against fat. "You may be a little overweight," she said, "but at least you have your health."

The Post-marketing Study of Prescription Drugs Is Not Adequate

David J. Graham

David J. Graham has spent more than twenty years researching drug safety at the Food and Drug Administration (FDA). He made headlines as a whistleblower in 2004 when he testified before the Senate Finance Committee, exposing the dangers of the pain medication Vioxx and alleging the inability of the FDA to protect the public from unsafe drugs.

E*ditor's Note: The following viewpoint is taken from congressional testimony given by the author before the U.S. Senate Committee on Finance.*

Let me begin by describing what we found in our study, what others have found, and what this means for the American people. Prior to approval of Vioxx, a study was performed by Merck named 090. This study found nearly a 7-fold increase in heart attack risk with low dose Vioxx. The labeling at approval said nothing about heart attack risks. In November 2000, another Merck clinical trial named VIGOR found a 5-fold increase in heart attack risk with high-dose Vioxx. The company said the drug was safe and that the comparison drug naproxen, was protective. In 2002, a large epidemiologic study reported a 2-fold increase in heart attack risk with high-dose Vioxx and another study reported that naproxen did not affect heart attack risk. About 18 months after the VIGOR results were published, FDA [the U.S. Food and Drug Administration] made a labeling change about heart attack risk with high-dose Vioxx, but did not place this in the "Warnings" section. Also, it did not ban the high-dose formulation and its

David J. Graham, testimony before the U.S. Senate Committee on Finance, November 18, 2004. www.senate.gov.

use. I believe such a ban should have been implemented. Of note, FDA's label change had absolutely no effect on how often high-dose Vioxx was prescribed, so what good did it achieve?

We are faced with what may be the single greatest drug safety catastrophe in the history of this country or the history of the world.

In March of 2004, another epidemiologic study reported that both high-dose and low-dose Vioxx increased the risk of heart attacks compared to Vioxx's leading competitor, Celebrex. Our study, first reported in late August of [2004], found that Vioxx increased the risk of heart attack and sudden death by 3.7-fold for high-dose and 1.5-fold for low-dose, compared to Celebrex. A study report describing this work was put on the FDA website on election day. Among many things, this report estimated that nearly 28,000 excess cases of heart attack or sudden cardiac death were caused by Vioxx. I emphasize to the Committee that this is an extremely conservative estimate. FDA always claims that randomized clinical trials provide the best data. If you apply the risk-levels seen in the 2 Merck trials, VIGOR and APPROVe [the latter done in 2001], you obtain a more realistic and likely range of estimates for the number of excess cases in the US. This estimate ranges from 88,000 to 139,000 Americans. Of these, 30–40% probably died. For the survivors, their lives were changed forever. It's important to note that this range does not depend at all on the data from our Kaiser-FDA study. Indeed, Dr. Eric Topol at the Cleveland Clinic recently estimated up to 160,000 cases of heart attacks and strokes due to Vioxx, in an article published in the *New England Journal of Medicine*. This article lays out clearly the public health significance of what we're talking about today.

So, how many people is 100,000?. . . We're not just talking numbers. For example, if we were talking about Florida or Pennsylvania, 1% of the entire State population would have been affected. For Iowa, it would be 5%, for Maine, 10% and for Wyoming, 27%. . . .

But there is another way to put this range of excess cases into perspective. Imagine that instead of a serious side-effect of a widely used prescription drug, we were talking about jet-liners. Please ignore the obvious difference in fatality rates between a heart attack and a plane crash, and focus on the larger analogy I'm trying to draw. If there were an average of 150 to 200 people on an aircraft, this range of 88,000 to 138,000 would be the rough equivalent of 500 to 900 aircraft dropping from the sky. This translates to 2–4 aircraft every week, week in and week out, for the past 5 years. If you were confronted by this situation, what would be your reaction, what would you want to know and what would you do about it?

Brief History of U.S. Drug Disasters

Another way to fully comprehend the enormity of the Vioxx debacle is to look briefly at recent US and FDA history. . . . In 1938, Congress enacted the Food, Drug and Cosmetic Act [FD&C Act], basically creating the FDA, in response to an unfortunate incident in which about 100 children were killed by elixir of sulfanilamide, a medication that was formulated using anti-freeze. This Act required that animal toxicity testing be performed and safety information be submitted to FDA prior to approval of a drug. In 1962, Congress enacted the Kefauver-Harris Amendments to the FD&C Act, in response to the thalidomide disaster in Europe. Overseas, between 1957 and 1961, an estimated 5,000 to 10,000 children were born with thalidomide-related birth defects. These Amendments increased the requirements for toxicity testing and safety information pre-approval, and added the requirement that "substantial evidence" of efficacy be submitted. Today, in 2004, you, we, are faced with what may be the single greatest drug safety catastrophe in the history of this country or the history of the world. We are talking about a catastrophe that I strongly believe could have, should have been largely or completely avoided. But it wasn't, and over 100,000 Americans have paid dearly for this failure. In my opinion, the FDA has let the American people down, and sadly, betrayed a public trust. . . .

My Vioxx Experience at FDA

To begin, after publication of the VIGOR study in November 2000, I became concerned about the potential public health risk that might exist with Vioxx. VIGOR suggested that the risk of heart attack was increased 5-fold in patients who used the high-dose strength of this drug. Why was the Vioxx safety question important? 1) Vioxx would undoubtedly be used by millions of patients. That's a very large number to expose to a serious drug risk. 2) Heart attack is a fairly common event, and 3) given the above, even a relatively small increase in heart attack risk due to Vioxx could mean that tens of thousands of Americans might be seriously harmed or killed by use of this drug. If these three factors were present, I knew that we would have all the ingredients necessary to guarantee a national disaster. The first two factors were established realities. It came down to the third factor, that is, what was the level of risk with Vioxx at low- and high-dose.

To get answers to this urgent issue, I worked with Kaiser Permanente in California to perform a large epidemiologic study. This study was carefully done and took nearly 3 years to complete. In early August of [2004], we completed our main analyses and assembled a poster presentation describing some of our more important findings. We had planned to present these data at the International Conference on Pharmacoepidemiology, in Bordeaux, France. We concluded that high-dose Vioxx significantly increased the risk of heart attacks and sudden death and that the high doses of the drug should not be prescribed or used by patients. This conclusion triggered an explosive response from the Office of New Drugs [OND] which approved Vioxx in the first place and was responsible for regulating it post-marketing. The response from senior management in my Office, the Office of Drug Safety [ODS] was equally stressful. I was pressured to change my conclusions and recommendations, and basically threatened that if I did not change them, I would not be permitted to present the paper at the conference. . . .

There were 2 other revelatory milestones. In mid-August, despite our study results showing an increased risk of heart attack with Vioxx, and despite the results of other studies published in the literature, FDA announced it had approved Vioxx for use in children with rheumatoid arthritis. Also, on September 22, at a meeting attended by the director of the re-viewing office that approved Vioxx, the director and deputy director of the reviewing division within that office and senior managers from the Office of Drug Safety, no one thought there was a Vioxx safety issue to be dealt with. At this meet-ing, the reviewing office director asked why had I even thought to study Vioxx and heart attacks because FDA had made its labeling change and nothing more needed to be done. At this meeting a senior manager from ODS labeled our Vioxx study "a scientific rumor." Eight days later, Merck pulled Vioxx from the market. . . .

Past Experiences

My experience with Vioxx is typical of how CDER [the Center for Drug Evaluation and Research] responds to serious drug safety issues in general. This is similar to what Dr. [Andrew] Mosholder went through when he reached his conclusion that most SSRIs [selective serotonin reuptake inhibitors, such as Vioxx] should not be used by children. I could bore you with a long list of prominent and not-so-prominent safety issues where CDER and its Office of New Drugs proved to be extremely resistant to full and open disclosure of safety information, especially when it called into question an existing regulatory position. In these situations, the new drug reviewing division that approved the drug in the first place and that regards it as its own child, typically proves to be the single greatest obstacle to effectively dealing with serious drug safety issues. The second greatest obstacle is often the senior management within the Office of Drug Safety, who either actively or tacitly go along with what the Office of New Drugs wants. Examples are numerous so I'll mention just a few.

With Lotronex, even though there was strong evidence in the pre-approval clinical trials of a problem with ischemic colitis, OND approved it. When cases of severe constipation and ischemic colitis began pouring into FDA's MedWatch program, the reaction was one of denial. . . .

Vioxx is a terrible tragedy and a profound regulatory failure.

Rezulin was a drug used to treat diabetes. It also caused acute liver failure, which was usually fatal unless a liver transplant was performed. The pre-approval clinical trials showed strong evidence of liver toxicity. The drug was withdrawn from the market in the United Kingdom in December 1997. With CDER and the Office of New Drugs, withdrawal didn't occur until March 2000. Between these dates, CDER relied on risk management strategies that were utterly ineffective and it persisted in relying on these strategies long after the evidence was clear that they didn't work. The continued marketing of Rezulin probably led to thousands of Americans being severely injured or killed by the drug. And note, there were many other safer diabetes drugs available. During this time, I understand that Rezulin's manufacturer continued to make about $2 million per day in sales.

The Big Picture

The problem you are confronting today is immense in scope. Vioxx is a terrible tragedy and a profound regulatory failure. I would argue that the FDA, as currently configured, is incapable of protecting America against another Vioxx. We are virtually defenseless.

It is important that this Committee and the American people understand that what has happened with Vioxx is really a symptom of something far more dangerous to the safety of the American people. Simply put, FDA and its Center for Drug Evaluation and Research are broken. . . .

[The Center for Drug Evaluation and Research] views the pharmaceutical industry it is supposed to regulate as its client.

The organizational structure within CDER is entirely geared towards the review and approval of new drugs, When a CDER new drug reviewing division approves a new drug, it is also saying the drug is "safe and effective." When a serious safety issue arises post-marketing, their immediate reaction is almost always one of denial, rejection and heat. They approved the drug so there can't possibly be anything wrong with it. The same group that approved the drug is also responsible for taking regulatory action against it post-marketing. This is an inherent conflict of interest. At the same time, the Office of Drug Safety has no regulatory power and must first convince the new drug reviewing division that a problem exists before anything beneficial to the public can be done. Often, the new drug reviewing division is the single greatest obstacle to effectively protecting the public against drug safety risks. A close second in my opinion, is an ODS management that sees its mission as pleasing the Office of New Drugs.

The corporate culture within CDER is also a barrier to effectively protecting the American people from unnecessary harm due to prescription and OTC [over-the-counter] drugs. The culture is dominated by a world-view that believes only randomized clinical trials provide useful and actionable information and that post-marketing safety is an afterthought. This culture also views the pharmaceutical industry it is supposed to regulate as its client, over-values the benefits of the drugs it approves and seriously under-values, disregards and disrespects drug safety.

Faulty Scientific Standards

Finally, the scientific standards CDER applies to drug safety guarantee that unsafe and deadly drugs will remain on the US market. When an OND reviewing division reviews a drug to decide whether to approve it, great reliance is placed on statistical tests. Usually, a drug is only approved if there is a 95% or greater probability that the drug actually works. From a safety perspective, this is also a very protective standard because it protects patients against drugs that don't work. The real problem is how CDER applies statistics to post-marketing safety. We see from the structural and cultural problems in CDER, that everything revolves around OND and the drug approval process.

When it comes to safety, the OND paradigm of 95% certainty prevails. Under this paradigm, a drug is safe until you can show with 95% or greater certainty that it is not safe. This is an incredibly high, almost insurmountable barrier to overcome. It's the equivalent of "beyond a shadow of a doubt." And here's an added kicker. In order to demonstrate a safety problem with 95% certainty, extremely large studies are often needed. And guess what. Those large studies can't be done.

There are 2 analogies I want to leave you with to illustrate the unreasonableness of CDER's standard of evidence as applied to safety, both pre- and post-approval. If the weatherman says there is an 80% chance of rain, most people would bring an umbrella. Using CDER's standard, you wouldn't bring an umbrella until there was a 95% or greater chance of rain. The second analogy is more graphic, but I think it brings home the point more clearly. Imagine for a moment that you have a pistol with a barrel having 100 chambers. Now, randomly place 95 bullets into those chambers. The gun represents a drug and the bullets represent a serious safety problem. Using CDER's standard, only when you have 95 bullets or more in the gun will you agree that the gun is loaded and a safety problem exists. Let's remove 5 bullets at random. We now have 90 bullets distributed across 100 chambers. Because there is only a 90% chance that a bullet will fire when I pull the trigger, CDER would conclude that the gun is not loaded and that the drug is safe.

Excessive Caution in Drug Approval Causes More Harm than It Prevents

Scott Gottlieb

Scott Gottlieb is a practicing physician and resident fellow at the American Enterprise Institute.

After three airplanes exploded over the last 11 years, the Federal Aviation Administration [FAA] isolated the problem, and settled on a budding solution. It is believed the blasts were a consequence of a combustible mix of fuel vapors that can fill gas tanks on hot days. To the FAA's critics, the agency was slow to uncover the culprit. To practical minds, the FAA was dealing with a remote problem and a rare effect.

The agency's solution is retrofitting airplanes with on-board "inerting systems" that pump nitrogen into fuel tanks. It lowers the amount of oxygen in fuel vapors and reduces their flammability. The new systems, at a quarter of a million each, cost a lot of money and fall short of guaranteeing more airplanes won't explode. But when it comes to air travel, this additional safety margin may be the best we can do, because we already made most of the easy fixes.

As the industry's safety record grows more superlative, ending infrequent crashes becomes both more difficult, and expensive.

We can make our drug development system a little safer, but only at a very big cost.

The same is true of prescription drugs, which like airlines, is one of the most regulated industries in the country. Over

Scott Gottlieb, "The Price of Too Much Caution," *New York Sun*, December 22, 2004. www.aei.org. Reproduced by permission.

the last 50 years, we have added successive layers of testing and monitoring before new drugs are approved for sale to patients, to the point where the average development time for a new drug can span 10 years and cost almost $1 billion.

The result is that today we have the safest system in the world, but few glaring gaps to easily improve on. When it comes to making new drugs safer, most of the obvious solutions are already accounted for and we have reached the flat part of a curve that measures incremental safety against the additional cost. We can make our drug development system a little safer, but only at a very big cost.

A Trade-Off

This trade-off is at issue, after the pain medications Vioxx and Celebrex, known as Cox-2 inhibitors, were traced to small but higher risks of heart attacks among patients who use them. Drugs like Vioxx are called Cox-2 inhibitors because they selectively inhibit pathways that cause pain but, unlike similar painkillers like Advil, the Cox-2s do not block pathways in the body that also produce chemicals that protect the tummy lining.

Based on these concerns, the drug company Merck pulled its drug Vioxx from the market. The maker of Celebrex has taken a more cautious approach while it investigates the potential link, suspending promotion of its drug while investing in studies to separate fact from theory.

The benefit of an off chance of discovering a rare side effect before a new drug is approved is eventually outweighed by the cost of keeping promising drugs from patients.

That approach may have been vindicated ... when the FDA announced that the agency also discovered a link between heart attacks and the common over-the-counter drug

Naproxen, an older close cousin of the Cox 2s, raising the specter that the higher heart-attack risk may extend to this entire class of painkillers. The side effect may eventually emerge as a fact of life when it comes to these painkillers, and another trade-off that doctors and patients need to weigh.

Consumers are angry that these problems were not unearthed earlier. But the higher risk of heart attacks caused by Vioxx, for example, was on the order of about six or seven heart attacks for every 1,000 patients who took the drug. In an older-patient population that already suffered more heart attacks, such a risk could have been easily missed, even with a clinical trial that included 10,000 patients or more. With this additional testing, the benefit of an off chance of discovering a rare side effect before a new drug is approved is eventually outweighed by the cost of keeping promising drugs from patients.

The Price of Too Much Caution

Even delaying seemingly ordinary drugs can have dramatic consequences on the public health. The first non-sedating anti-allergy medicine, Claritin, took almost seven years to get approved, while sleepy drivers with sniffles continued to cause car accidents. Each of the popular anti-cholesterol drugs known as statins that today prevent 15 percent to 30 percent of heart attacks took several years to get approved. How many people died waiting? The math is straightforward.

Or consider this math: It's estimated more than 20,000 people died between 1985 and 1987 waiting for streptokinase, the first drug that could be intravenously administered to re-open the blocked coronary arteries of heart attack victims. Between 1988 and 1992, about 3,500 kidney cancer patients died waiting for Interleukin-2, which was available in several European countries. In 1988 alone, it is estimated between 7,500 and 15,000 people died from gastric ulcers caused by aspirin and other non-steroidal anti-inflammatory drugs, waiting for the FDA to approve misoprostol, which was already available in 43 countries.

This is the price of too much caution, when drugs are held hostage to safety testing with lethal consequences. The poisonous compromise is becoming the prevailing orthodoxy inside the FDA right now [in late 2004], as the agency understandably withdraws under the withering attacks from a sound-bite-obsessed Congress and headline-hungry press.

The effects of this deadly atmosphere can already be seen in the FDA's decision . . . to delay approval of a promising cancer drug, Marqibo, for the treatment of aggressive non-Hodgkin's lymphoma. This go-slow approach was also apparent in the lopsided vote to withhold approval of the testosterone patch for women, being touted as the "Viagra for women." That decision was driven by theoretical fears of certain risks rather than problems already manifest.

Some have estimated that pumping nitrogen into gas tanks will save about one plane from crashing over the next 25 years. To many people, this is a fair price to pay, especially if you happen to be on that one plane when it is ready to blow. To others, it is a big price to stamp out a remote risk. When it comes to new drugs, the returns on our newfound caution may be even less striking.

Panic over Prescription-Drug Risks Leads People to Stop Taking Needed Medication

Irene S. Levine

Irene S. Levine is a writer and journalist who was formerly a senior policy maker at the National Institute of Mental Health.

When the pain reliever Vioxx was withdrawn from the market last fall [2004] after the announcement that it increased patients' risk of heart attacks and strokes, millions of Americans panicked. The sometimes-sensationalized headlines didn't help: People wondered, Should I trust my doctor? Could a medication that I thought would help me actually kill me? Is our drug safety system broken?

Suddenly, ads for the drug were replaced with ads looking for Vioxx "victims." Law firms across the nation began recruiting anyone who had ever taken the drug as plaintiffs for class-action suits. Merck, the company that developed the drug, could be liable for billions of dollars, making it one of the costliest liability cases ever. No surprise, then, that Merck's stock plummeted 40 percent in just six weeks.

But the real cost was even greater: Not only did patients stop taking Vioxx but, doctors say, many people stopped taking their other medicines, too—sometimes putting their health at serious risk.

Vioxx was the first pebble in the pharmaceutical rock slide. Soon, accusations about a spate of other drugs were making headlines, including all COX-2 inhibitors which, like Vioxx, relieve pain. The charges didn't stop there. The FDA [Food and Drug Administration] was accused of simply rubber-stamping new drugs; drug companies were blamed for hiding information about unsafe products; and the efficacy of clinical trials that did not reveal how large numbers of people would react was questioned. But one question that was rarely asked could determine whether or not pharmaceutical companies continue to develop and produce breakthrough medications that can save or extend lives and help people live without pain. The question: Do Americans expect drugs to be risk-free? And, if someone suffers a bad reaction, will lawyers rather than doctors be the first people we call?

Panic over Pills: Overreaction?

During the ten-year period between 1994 and 2004, the FDA approved 321 completely new drugs (this doesn't include approvals for changes to existing medicines), bringing the total to more than 10,000 drug products on the market. During that same period, eight drugs were withdrawn for reasons of safety, such as the diet drug fenfluramine (fen-phen, associated with heart-valve disease) and the allergy drug Seldane (linked to heart arrhythmias). But the Vioxx recall created a shock wave for the American consumer like no other. Many people had come to depend on their "meds," and they expected them to be safe, too, especially when they cost so much. . . .

"With Vioxx, the real shock and outrage came when there was a suggestion that people in authority may have known about these harmful side effects and not shared them with doctors or the public," says Anne Woodbury, chief health advocate for the Center for Health Transformation, a think tank founded by [former Speaker of the House] Newt Gingrich. It made people question their faith in the pharmaceutical industry, federal regulators and physicians: those we trust to make sure our drugs are safe. Before, taking a newly prescribed pill with a slug of water was as routine as brushing your teeth. For many people, this is no longer the case.

"Now patients and doctors are going to ask themselves: Could this new drug be another Vioxx?," says Jerry Avorn, MD, a professor of medicine at Harvard Medical School and the author of *Powerful Medicines: The Benefits, Risks and Costs of Prescription Drugs*.

People have reason to worry. In clinical trial data submitted to the FDA, Vioxx showed no connection to heart problems. The drug was approved in May 1999. But after Vioxx hit the market and grew in popularity, heart problems were revealed—lots of them. Tens of thousands of people may have been affected, and Merck was accused of hiding that information.

As a society we expect medicine to be perfect. There is no such thing. There is always a risk.

"The system is not perfect," comments Marianne J. Legato, MD, professor of clinical medicine at Columbia University College of Physicians and Surgeons in New York City. "Sometimes a company may not want to show data that are negative till they really know what's going on. But it's ridiculous to suggest that they would suppress things willy-nilly, because if a drug is going to cause severe side effects, it's not in their best interest to hide that."

Too Many Variables

Legato, who has a busy practice in internal medicine, continues, "All this hysteria is ridiculous. We're putting the pharmaceutical industry under a microscope in a completely inappropriate way. Americans have somehow come to believe they should get the best medical care with the latest remedies with no side effects. Well, guess what? There is no drug that doesn't have side effects."

Other experts say it's time for a major reality check. "With all due respect, I think the press has made this into a firestorm," says Peter Corr, PhD, head of worldwide research and development for drug manufacturer Pfizer. "As a society we expect medicine to be perfect. There is no such thing. There is always a risk."

Even when a side effect is suspected, it can be very difficult to prove that it was directly caused by the drug. "With some kinds of adverse reactions, like liver toxicity, it's fairly obvious that it's related to the drug," says Robert Temple, MD, director of the office of medical policy at the FDA's Center for Drug Evaluation and Research. "But it's much more difficult to link a heart attack or a stroke, because these are very common in the population. If someone has a heart attack, what would even make you imagine that the drug did it?"

Despite the risks, there's no need to panic about prescriptions.

There are so many variables, any one of which could cause an adverse reaction to a drug, from taking an incorrect dose to combining the drug with other medicines. A growing cause of concern is the trend toward self-medication with untested OTC [over-the-counter] supplements. If, for instance, a patient is taking an herbal remedy and also takes a painkiller or an antidepressant, what will the combined effect be?

Despite the risks, there's no need to panic about prescriptions, says Temple. "Of drugs that are approved, about one or two percent may be withdrawn eventually. It's rare." And if you have enough information to weigh the risks and benefits, you and your doctor can make an informed decision.

How Side Effects Emerge

How can dangerous side effects take years, or even decades, to become known? A new drug is first tested on animals. If the results indicate that it's likely to be both safe and effective, the company applies to the FDA for permission to begin testing it in humans. Human studies have three phases: to evaluate safety, to determine effectiveness, and to verify safety, dosage and effectiveness. Although a trial may extend as long as five years and often includes between 3,000 and 10,000 people, each participant may only receive the medication for a period of weeks or months. Statistically, rare and dangerous side effects may not emerge until millions of people have used the drug, after FDA approval.

So why don't we test drugs on more people and for longer periods of time? For one thing, quicker approvals may save lives, as with drugs for AIDS or a vaccine for a newly emerging flu pandemic. Another reason is cost. "It already costs a billion dollars to get a drug from an idea to the market," says Corr. "If we had to study a million patients before we took a drug to market, there would never be another drug."

Monitoring After Approval

After a drug is approved, it is subject to post-market surveillance. The FDA analyzes reports of "adverse events," or drug side effects, which come from the industry, from ongoing clinical trials and through its MedWatch program, to which consumers, physicians, pharmacists and other health professionals voluntarily report problems.

Negative reports about a drug that's on the market can yield crucial new information. "Clinical trials that are negative are, many times, just as important as the trials that show positive results," says Marvin Lipman, MD, chief medical adviser for *Consumer Reports*. Legislation was introduced in both the House and Senate in October 2004 to establish a registry of all clinical trials and their results (clinicaltrials.gov). "We are the most regulated industry in the world," says Corr. "And frankly, that's how it should be. If there is a problem with a drug, we want to know about it sooner rather than later."

Consumers may know sooner too. In February [2005] the FDA announced the creation of an independent Drug Safety

Oversight Board to provide expanded and faster drug-safety information to doctors and patients. While there will always be risks, the public may be better equipped to judge and act on them.

"We still need to be willing to take personal responsibility for assessing the risk-benefit ratio of a medication," says Legato. "Yes, you have to be completely informed to do it. And, yes, it's complex. But if we don't do this, it's like going back to the Middle Ages when there were no risks, except of dying by the age of 26. We have nearly doubled life expectancy since the beginning of the 20th century. That did not happen by accident. Prescription drugs have played a huge role."

Safety Concerns About Prescription Drugs Are Exaggerated and Will Result in Higher Prices

Henry I. Miller

Henry I. Miller is a physician and a fellow at Stanford University's Hoover Institution. He was a Food and Drug Administration official from 1979 to 1994, and is the author of The Frankenfood Myth.

The Food and Drug Administration [FDA] lately has been trying to demonstrate to its critics that it really, really, really takes drug safety seriously. In fact, no one familiar with the FDA's culture and mind-set could possibly doubt that to regulators drug safety is paramount—if for no other reason, approving a product that proves dangerous can destroy a government career.

Although all drugs have side effects—which can be serious and/or frequent—modern pharmaceuticals have never been safer, more effective, more innovative—or more stringently regulated. But that seems to have escaped the notice of many members of Congress. Various senators have introduced two separate bills that will further obstruct innovation and threaten public health.

Sens. Edward Kennedy, Massachusetts Democrat, and Michael Enzi, Wyoming Republican, the chairman and ranking Republican, respectively, of the Health, Education, Labor and Pensions Committee, proposed legislation to grant the FDA new authority to impose safety requirements on medicines after their approval for marketing and would also require registration of clinical trials and the reporting of their results in public databases.

In addition, Sens. Chris Dodd, Connecticut Democrat, and Charles Grassley, Iowa Republican, introduced legislation to create within the FDA a center to oversee the safety of drugs after they go on the market.

These bills are the culmination of years of drug company–bashing by a small number of activists and members of Congress who have seized on high-profile events such as deficiencies in the labeling of antidepressants and the discovery of previously unknown side effects of various widely used drugs. They will discourage drug development by making it more difficult and expensive and less profitable. This at a time when an aging American population desperately needs new and improved (and cheaper) medicines, and when pharmaceutical R&D [research and development] is already ailing.

The trends are ominous: The length of clinical testing for the average drug is increasing, fewer drugs are approved and the number of industry applications to FDA for marketing approval has been declining for more than a decade. Unsurprisingly, in the last 20 years, development costs skyrocketed, with direct and indirect expenses now exceeding $900 million to bring an average drug to market.

Not surprisingly, those costs have been passed along: [In March 2007], the AARP [a nonprofit membership organization of persons 50 and older] reported a 6.2 percent rise in the manufacturer list price for 193 brand-name prescription drugs and 75 generic prescription drugs commonly used by adults aged 50 and older. That's almost double the nation's overall inflation rate of 3.2 percent in 2006.

The FDA is already the nation's most powerful and omnipresent regulator, but the Kennedy-Enzi bill would grant new authority, supposedly to ensure the safety of drugs. Among other unwise innovations, it would require the imposition of "risk management action plans" (RiskMAPs) when drugs are approved. Not only does the FDA already have the authority to require these when regulators feel that they are necessary, but they have been overused and abusive: At times the exhaustive (and exhausting) list of requirements for physicians, pharmacists and patients seems more appropriate for weapons-grade plutonium than a pharmaceutical.

Nothing in our society is more stringently regulated and monitored than drug development.

The requirement that drug companies disclose advanced clinical trials in a public database is based on concerns that "negative" results are often obscured or simply not reported. It is intended to prevent companies from "cherry picking" studies, divulging only those that yield favorable results and suppressing the rest.

These concerns are exaggerated. Nothing in our society is more stringently regulated and monitored than drug development. During each phase of clinical testing, the FDA reviews and must grant permission for every clinical trial and has access to all the proprietary information about the drug. When the manufacturer has accumulated evidence the drug is safe and effective, as part of the application for marketing approval the results of every trial and everything else known about the drug, both in the United States and abroad, must be reported to the FDA.

Statistical analysis must be performed in an appropriate and prespecified manner. Moreover, the FDA serves as a repository for data on similar drugs made by other manufacturers. All of this prevents statistical "cherry picking" or "data mining" that could mislead regulators.

There is also the question of the meaning of "negative results" in clinical trials. In the context of scientific and clinical experiments, the term has a meaning very different from the common usage. Such trials are seldom "negative" in the sense of revealing the drug tested inflicts harm but, for various reasons, they may not be useful or applicable to the indications (uses) for which approval is being sought. The reasons can include: insufficient statistical power (that is, number of patients) in the study; inappropriate choice of route, dose or frequency of administration, or in the stratification of subjects; or simply a failure of the drug to be effective for the indication for which it was tried.

The Dodd-Grassley proposal is even worse. It would create within the FDA an antidrug entity with strong incentives to argue for the nonapproval or withdrawal from the market of drugs that have significant side effects even if they offer huge net benefits. (We have seen this already from certain factions within the agency.)

These proposed legislative remedies for the FDA's problems, with more planned for later in the year in both the House and Senate, are analogous to the discredited medical practice of bleeding the patient with leeches. By intensifying the FDA's notorious risk aversion, the new measures will inflate even further the costs, difficulty and uncertainty of drug development and reduce the number of drug candidates that begin and complete clinical testing. They will drain the life's blood from innovation and inflict harm on patients.

The Lengthy Approval Process for Prescription Drugs Costs Lives

Gilbert L. Ross

Gilbert L. Ross is a physician and coeditor of the American Council on Science and Health booklet Weighing Benefits and Risks in Pharmaceutical Use.

An aphorism never truer: when discussing breast cancer, an ounce of prevention is better for public health than the cures currently available, and much cheaper. So, after a long-and-winding eight-year period of data accumulation, we should applaud the FDA [U.S. Food and Drug Administration] for finally approving [pharmaceuticals giant Eli] Lilly's "designer estrogen," Evista (raloxifene), for use in postmenopausal high-risk women to lower their risk of invasive breast cancer. But we should question why the FDA took this long in the first place.

As of Friday the 14th [of September, 2007], the drug, more scientifically termed a selective estrogen receptor modulator (SERM), also got FDA approval for cancer chemoprevention in postmenopausal women with osteoporosis (it has been available for osteoporosis prevention and treatment since 1999). Chemoprevention is the prescription of medication to lower the risk of a disease or condition from which the patient does not yet suffer but for which she is of higher susceptibility. In this case, women at high risk would take Evista as an agent of chemoprevention of breast cancer.

Until now, tamoxifen was the only FDA-approved drug to lower the risk of breast cancer, although neither it nor Evista is a panacea [cure-all]. While studies vary, in general these drugs reduce the risk by about one-half: in other words, if the rate of breast cancer is 8 per thousand, those taking a chemo-preventive drug lower the risk to 4 per thousand. So hundreds of high-risk women would be treated to prevent only a few cancers. Also, like all drugs, these have their risks: both drugs can produce vein disease, including clots, and there is a higher risk of stroke.

Benefit May Outweigh Risk

So is Evista a real benefit or a potentially "dangerous drug?" The answer here depends on a careful assessment of the individual benefits and the risks. The increased risk of phlebitis (clots) or stroke is quite small, but any woman with a history of venous disease, or an increased risk of stroke, would be well advised to avoid these drugs—unless the doctor and patient find the benefits outweigh the risks.

Excess caution in drug approval takes lives—as does the FDA's exceedingly long learning curve on "off-label" uses of existing medicines.

The key is figuring out how much breast cancer risk a woman really has. An individual's criteria can be entered into a standardized decision key to make her risk clearer, though of course not certain. Factors influencing a woman's risk include: age, family history, menstrual onset, age at first pregnancy, alcohol intake, and obesity, among several others. After all the relevant factors are recorded, if her breast cancer risk is significantly elevated, she may be a candidate to take a chemo-prevention drug. In the near future, it may be possible for personalized genetic evaluation to increase the accuracy of our risk prediction significantly.

There are other drugs for which there is evidence of a reduction in breast cancer risk, but large-scale studies have not yet been completed, so they have not been FDA-approved for that purpose. These are the aromatase inhibitors, and they work by interfering with the production of estrogen in breast tissue. They have been shown to work well to help reduce the spread of cancer already detected, and preliminary work regarding their use in chemoprevention has also yielded some encouraging results.

Let's hope that the aromatase inhibitor studies can be completed, and evaluated, much faster than the seven-plus years it took the FDA to bestow its seal of approval on raloxifene. Early studies published in 1998 and 1999 seemed to show that raloxifene markedly reduced breast cancer risk, but only now has FDA approval arrived.

A Long Delay Should Not Be Necessary

Why the long delay? One major reason is the increased scrutiny given to new drug applications in the current risk-averse, "safety first" FDA. Until raloxifene was shown to be at least as safe and effective as the older tamoxifen—which was accomplished by the publication of the Study of Tamoxifen And Raloxifene (STAR) trial in June 2006—it was clear that approval would not be forthcoming. Nowadays, FDA's implicit rule seems to be that a new drug will not only have to be good, it will have to be better than the older drugs available.

Such a standard applies to no other industry—why should it apply to life-saving pharmaceuticals, given that a variety of drug options may increase the odds of helping diverse patients? Or, to put it another way, how many women were prevented from benefiting from this useful new drug during the years before FDA approval?

When a drug is not FDA-approved, even if doctors have heard of it, they are reluctant to prescribe it, in part out of fear of lawsuits. Many doctors are also fearful now of new drugs, given the recent heightened publicity about side effects from drugs like Vioxx and Avandia. Also, insurance companies often will not reimburse patients for drugs prescribed "off-label" [i.e., for a condition not originally intended to be treated by it].

Given the still-tragic toll that breast cancer takes upon American women, we need all the effective therapies we can get to reduce the risk. Excess caution in drug approval takes lives—as does the FDA's exceedingly long learning curve on "off-label" uses of existing medicines. Former FDA Commissioner David Kessler has said that "we have to find creative ways of getting [new] cancer drugs to patients even if we end up being wrong a few times." Kessler is right, but is anyone at the FDA listening?

Terminally Ill Patients Should Be Allowed to Use Experimental Drugs

Sigrid Fry-Revere

Sigrid Fry-Revere is director of bioethics studies at the Cato Institute, a nonprofit public policy foundation in Washington, D.C., that supports free markets, limited government, and individual liberty.

Jolee Mohr died in July [2007] at the age of 36 after receiving experimental treatment for arthritis. "It was supposed to be just a simple thing," said her husband, Robb, but something went horribly wrong.

"No one knows yet whether the treatment was to blame," wrote Rick Weiss of the *Washington Post*. "But a close look at the events leading to Mohr's death reveals failures in the safety net that is supposed to protect people from the risks of medical experimentation."

[In early August 2007], the U.S. Court of Appeals for the District of Columbia ruled that terminally ill patients do not have a constitutional right to use experimental treatments without being enrolled in a clinical trial or participating in other very limited Food and Drug Administration–approved options, even if their doctors believe that such treatment is their best chance for survival. The case is being appealed to the Supreme Court.

The [District of Columbia] appeals court and so many others who share a "safety first" approach to experimental treatment are only seeing half the picture. Experimental treatment is inherently risky. But overemphasizing safety prevents patients from taking a calculated risk when they think it's worthwhile.

Sigrid Fry-Revere, "When It's Life or Death, Who Makes the Call?" *Los Angeles Times*, August 15, 2007. Reproduced by permission.

As my husband and I learned, that freedom is important. Our son was diagnosed with cancer when he was 9 months old. Next week, he leaves for college, and the only visible reminder of his brush with death is a scar from surgery.

No, I'm not saying that an experimental treatment saved his life. What probably saved him was his parents' persistent questions, and events resulting in a course of treatment that changed so often no doctor would have recommended it at the beginning.

Individuals often react unexpectedly even to conventional treatments, let alone experimental ones. What would have happened if someone had told us, "Sorry, that treatment is no longer an option. It has been found unsafe because children have died from it."

At the time, all the treatments—including the experimental ones we were offered but ended up not choosing—resulted in about a 50% chance of death, and in many cases they killed the children before the cancer did. But there were still crucial choices to make. No one was as well suited to make them as we were, in consultation with our son's doctors.

In the appeals court case, the Abigail Alliance for Better Access to Developmental Drugs sued the FDA [U.S. Food and Drug Administration] for refusing to allow terminally ill patients to purchase experimental drugs. Patients who couldn't gain access to the medicines they wanted—because the trials were closed or the patients were too sick or otherwise didn't qualify for FDA permission—petitioned the FDA to be allowed to take medicines under the supervision of their own doctors.

According to the FDA, such treatments would lead to unacceptable risk.

Unacceptable to whom?

Patients Should Have the Right to Weigh Risks

In denying patients the right to weigh the risks for themselves, the FDA and the court denied them their only hope for survival. The government essentially told them that it would be better for them to do nothing and die than to take risky experimental treatments.

We do not need a governmental authority involved in medical decisions that are uniquely personal to patients and their families. But along with the right to make decisions comes the obligation to think them through. Any doctor who lies to patients or intentionally misleads them about the risks of certain treatments should be punished, but patients need to read informed-consent forms carefully, ask questions and not assume that their doctors can do risk-benefit analyses without knowing what's most important to the patient.

In our case, each option had its own set of risks, including death, but also a chance at a better life. One experimental protocol we were offered tested a new course of chemotherapy that had a lower chance of stunting our son's growth or causing sterility, but possibly also a lower chance of curing his cancer. But at least we had this option.

I wonder if in this "safety first" climate toward experimental treatment—and with this latest court ruling—any of the protocols we considered would be approved. All had the possibility of deadly side effects. It's frightening to think a government agency might have limited our options because it thought one treatment safer than another.

The proper response to tragedies like the one that befell Jolee Mohr is not to try to make experiments risk-free, but to help patients understand the risks.

Robb Mohr told the *Post* that "the science seemed good. There's nothing I knew of that could have predicted this." But the consent form his wife signed stated that the experimental therapy had possible "unknown side effects" including "in rare circumstances, death."

Participating in experimental treatments is a decision not to be taken lightly. If the public goes along with the "safety first" mentality and abdicates decision-making authority to government regulators, we will lose an important right. We'll lose the choice to participate in experiments that might kill us, but we'll also lose the option to make a choice that might save our lives.

CHAPTER 2

Do Pharmaceutical Companies Promote Unnecessary Drugs?

Direct-to-Consumer Prescription Drug Advertising: An Overview

Carol Rados

Carol Rados is a writer and editor for the U.S. Food and Drug Administration (FDA).

You may have seen the advertisement: A melodrama of crime and corruption, conflict and emotion, centering on indoor hit men like dust and dander, and outdoor hit men such as pollen and ragweed, all threatening to offend a young and very beautiful woman's nose. The 45-second broadcast ad covers everything from talking to your doctor to the possible side effects that people can expect. Then the narrator mentions "Flonase."

Entertaining though it may be, the Food and Drug Administration says this promotional piece about nasal allergy relief also has all the elements of a well-crafted, easy-to-understand prescription drug advertisement directed at consumers, and it meets agency requirements for these ads.

Direct-to-consumer (DTC) advertising of prescription drugs in its varied forms—TV, radio, magazines, newspapers—is widely used throughout the United States. DTC advertising is a category of promotional information about specific drug treatments provided directly to consumers by or on behalf of drug companies. According to the U.S. General Accounting [now called Accountability] Office—the investigational arm of Congress—pharmaceutical manufacturers spent $2.7 billion on DTC advertising in 2001 alone.

Carol Rados, "Truth in Advertising: Rx Drug Ads Come of Age," *FDA Consumer*, July/August 2004.

The Controversy

Whether it's a 1940s, detective-style film noir of unusual allergy suspects or a middle-aged man throwing a football through a tire swing announcing that he's "back in the game," the DTC approach to advertising prescription drugs has been controversial. Some say that DTC promotion provides useful information to consumers that results in better health outcomes. Others argue that it encourages overuse of prescription drugs and use of the most costly treatments, instead of less expensive treatments that would be just as satisfactory.

> [Direct-to-consumer] advertising . . . can help remove the stigma that accompanies diseases that in the past were rarely openly discussed.

There seems to be little doubt that DTC advertising can help advance the public health by encouraging more people to talk with health care professionals about health problems, particularly undertreated conditions such as high blood pressure and high cholesterol.

DTC advertising also can help remove the stigma that accompanies diseases that in the past were rarely openly discussed, such as erectile dysfunction or depression. DTC ads also can remind patients to get their prescriptions refilled and help them adhere to their medication regimens.

On the other hand, ads that are false or misleading do not advance—and may even threaten—the public health. While the FDA encourages DTC advertisements that contain accurate information, the agency also has the job of making sure that consumers are not misled or deceived by advertisements that violate the law.

"The goal here is getting truthful, non-misleading information to consumers about safe and effective therapeutic products so they can be partners in their own health care," says Peter Pitts, the FDA's associate commissioner for external relations. "Better-informed consumers are empowered to choose and use the products we regulate to improve their health."

How Ads Affect Consumers

The FDA surveyed both patients and physicians about their attitudes and experiences with DTC advertising between 1999 and 2002. The agency summarized the findings of these surveys in January 2003 in the report, *Assessment of Physician and Patient Attitudes Toward Direct-to-Consumer Promotion of Prescription Drugs*.

DTC advertising appears to influence certain types of behavior. For example, the FDA surveys found that among patients who visited doctors and asked about a prescription drug by brand name because of an ad they saw, 88 percent actually had the condition the drug treats. This is important, Pitts says, because physician visits that result in earlier detection of a disease combined with appropriate treatment, could mean that more people will live longer, healthier, more productive lives without the risk of future costly medical interventions.

[Direct-to-consumer] advertising may cultivate the belief among the public that there is a pill for every ill and contribute to the medicalization of trivial ailments.

With the number of ailments Patricia A. Sigler lives with—diabetes, fibromyalgia, high blood pressure, high cholesterol, nerve damage, and a heart defect called mitral valve prolapse—the 64-year-old small business owner in Jefferson, Md., says that she's always on the lookout for medicines that might improve her quality of life, and that she pays attention to DTC ads for prescription drugs.

Some Doctors Disagree

Michael S. Wilkes, M.D., vice dean of the medical school at the University of California, Davis, says that two reasons he doesn't like DTC advertising are that patients may withhold information from their doctors or try to treat themselves. Aiming prescription drug ads at consumers can affect the "dynamics of the patient-provider relationship," and ultimately, the patient's quality of care, Wilkes says. DTC advertising can motivate consumers to seek more information about a product or disease, but physicians need to help patients evaluate health-related information they obtain from DTC advertising, he says.

"DTC advertising may cultivate the belief among the public that there is a pill for every ill and contribute to the medicalization of trivial ailments, leading to an even more overmedicated society," Wilkes says. "Patients need to trust that I've got their best interest in mind."

Others who favor DTC ads say that consumer-directed information can be an important educational tool in a time when more patients want to be involved in their own health care. Carol Salzman, M.D., Ph.D., an internist in Chevy Chase, Md., emphasizes, however, that physicians still need to remain in control of prescribing medications.

"Doctors shouldn't feel threatened by their patients asking for a medicine by name," she says, "but at the same time, patients shouldn't come in expecting that a drug will be dispensed just because they asked for it."

[Direct-to-consumer] ads often masquerade as educational tools, but provide more promotion than education.

Salzman says she finds it time-consuming "trying to talk people out of something they have their hearts set on." Wilkes agrees. Discussions motivated by ads that focus on specific drugs or trivial complaints, he says, could take time away from subjects such as a patient's symptoms, the range of available treatments, and specific details about a patient's illness.

Education or Promotion?

At least one patient advocacy group is concerned about what it says are the downsides of advertising prescription drugs directly to consumers, claiming that DTC ads often masquerade as educational tools, but provide more promotion than education. The ads, they say, provide little access to unbiased information.

"People need to be careful with ads that it isn't just hype that they're going to feel better, with no objectivity of the downsides," says Linda Golodner, president of the National Consumers League in Washington, D.C. Although all DTC advertisements must disclose risk information, she says what is typically communicated is a brand name, a reason to use the product, and an impression of the product. Golodner wants all offices within the FDA that have a responsibility for any aspect of DTC advertising to work together. "There's a lot of the same information out there, so why not bring it all together so that consumers can understand it better?"...

DDMAC [the FDA's Division of Drug Marketing, Advertising and Communication] oversight helps ensure that pharmaceutical companies accurately communicate the benefits and risks of an advertised drug. The regulations require that advertising for prescription drugs must disclose certain information about the product's uses and risks.

In addition, advertisements cannot be false or misleading and cannot omit material facts. FDA regulations also call for "fair balance" in every product-claim ad. This means that the risks and benefits must be presented with comparable scope, depth, and detail, and that information relating to the product's effectiveness must be fairly balanced by risk information....

The Trouble with Ads

Of the three types of DTC advertisements, the first and most common—product-claim ads—mention a drug's name and the condition it is intended to treat, and describe the risks and benefits associated with taking the drug. Some manufacturers have decided not to present this much information and instead, have made use of two other kinds of ads. "Reminder" ads give only the name of the product, but not what it is used for, and "help-seeking" ads contain information about a disease, but do not mention a specific drug. These help-seeking—or disease-awareness—ads can be extremely informative and, because they name no drug, they are not regulated by the FDA. Examples of help-seeking ads are those that mention high cholesterol or diabetes, and then direct you to ask your doctor about treatments. Reminder ads call attention to a drug's name, but say nothing about the condition it is used to treat, its effectiveness, or safety information. A reminder ad is not required to include risk information.

There has been a great deal of discussion about the brief summary that accompanies DTC print ads. The typical brief summary is not brief and uses technical language. This is because it reprints all of the risk information from the physician labeling. People have complained that the brief summary cannot be understood by consumers. Aikin says, "Patients do not typically read the brief summary in DTC print ads unless they're interested in the product." Even then, she says, much information is likely glanced at, rather than fully read. . . .

For companies that don't follow the rules, DDMAC's possible actions include two types of letters—"untitled" and "warning.". . .

For example, the 60-second DTC broadcast television ad featuring "Digger," the well-known animated dermatophyte microorganism touting Lamisil (terbinafine), a treatment for nail fungus, was initially found to be false or misleading. The FDA sent an untitled letter to the makers of Lamisil for overstating the drug's effectiveness, minimizing its risk information, and making an unsubstantiated superiority claim. As a result, the manufacturer, Novartis Pharmaceuticals Corp., stopped running that ad.

DDMAC recently sent a warning letter to Bristol-Myers Squibb Co. about false or misleading promotional materials for Pravachol (pravastatin sodium), a drug approved to lower cholesterol in people with high cholesterol, to help prevent heart attacks in people with high cholesterol or heart disease, and to help prevent stroke in people with heart disease. One of the company's ads misleadingly suggested that the drug had been proven to help prevent stroke in all people worried about having a stroke, regardless of whether or not they had heart disease.

Another ad, directed at diabetes patients, misleadingly suggested that Pravachol had been proven to help prevent heart attacks and stroke in people with diabetes. Following the warning letter, the company created a corrective ad campaign acknowledging that Pravachol had not been approved for these indications.

Assessing DTC advertising is an on-going process for the FDA. As more research surfaces, the agency will continue to evaluate DTC drug promotion and will take additional measures as appropriate to protect the public health.

Pharmaceutical Companies Define Normal Conditions as Diseases

Ray Moynihan and Alan Cassels

Ray Moynihan is an internationally respected Australian journalist who specializes in medical issues. Alan Cassels is a pharmaceutical policy researcher at the University of Victoria in British Columbia and a commentator for Canadian news agencies.

Thirty years ago the head of one of the world's best-known drug companies made some very candid comments. Close to retirement at the time, Merck's aggressive chief executive Henry Gadsden told *Fortune* magazine of his distress that the company's potential markets had been limited to sick people. Suggesting he'd rather Merck to be more like chewing gum maker Wrigley's, Gadsen said it had long been his dream to make drugs for healthy people. Because then, Merck would be able to "sell to everyone." Three decades on, the late Henry Gadsden's dream has come true.

The marketing strategies of the world's biggest drug companies now aggressively target the healthy and the well. The ups and downs of daily life have become mental disorders, common complaints are transformed into frightening conditions, and more and more ordinary people are turned into patients. With promotional campaigns that exploit our deepest fears of death, decay, and disease, the $500 billion pharmaceutical industry is literally changing what it means to be human. Rightly rewarded for saving life and reducing suffering, the global drug giants are no longer content selling medicines only to the ill. Because, as Wall Street knows well, there's a lot of money to be made telling healthy people they're sick.

Ray Moynihan and Alan Cassels, "Prologue: Selling Sickness," *Selling Sickness: How the World's Biggest Pharmaceutical Companies Are Turning Us All into Patients*, New York: Nation Books, 2005, pp. ix–xviii.

Making Everyday Problems into Diseases

At a time when many of us are leading longer, healthier, and more vital lives than our ancestors, saturation advertising and slick "awareness-raising" campaigns are turning the worried well into the worried sick. Mild problems are painted as serious disease, so shyness becomes a sign of social anxiety disorder and premenstrual tension a mental illness called premenstrual dysphoric disorder. Everyday sexual difficulties are seen as sexual dysfunctions, the natural change of life is a disease of hormone deficiency called menopause, and distracted office workers now have adult ADD [attention deficit disorder]. Just being "at risk" of an illness has become a "disease" in its own right, so healthy middle-aged women now have a silent bone disease called osteoporosis, and fit middle-aged men a lifelong condition called high cholesterol.

With many health problems, there are people at the severe end of the spectrum suffering genuine illness, or at very high risk of it, who may benefit greatly from a medical label and a powerful medication. Yet for the relatively healthy people who are spread across the rest of the spectrum, a label and a drug may bring great inconvenience, enormous costs, and the very real danger of sometimes deadly side effects. This vast terrain has become the new global marketplace of potential patients— tens of millions of people—a key target of the drug industry's multibillion-dollar promotional budgets. . . .

Prescriptions for the most promoted categories, like heart medicines or antidepressants, have soared astronomically in the U.S., with the amount spent on these drugs doubling in less than five years. In many other nations the trend is also up. Young Australians took ten times more antidepressants in 2000 than they did in 1990. Canadian consumption of the new cholesterol-lowering drugs jumped by a staggering 300 percent over a similar time period. Many of those prescriptions enhanced or extended life. But there is a growing sense that too many of them are driven by the unhealthy influences of misleading marketing rather than genuine need. And those marketing strategies, like the drug companies, are now well and truly global.

Pharmaceutical companies now take the lead, not just in branding their blockbuster pills like Prozac and Viagra, but also in branding the conditions that create the markets for those pills.

Working from his midtown Manhattan office in New York City, Vince Parry represents the cutting edge of that global marketing. An expert in advertising, Parry now specializes in the most sophisticated form of selling medicines: he works with drug companies to help create new diseases. In an astonishing article titled "The art of branding a condition," Parry recently revealed the ways in which companies are involved in "fostering the creation" of medical disorders. Sometimes a little-known condition is given renewed attention, sometimes an old disease is redefined and renamed, and sometimes a whole new dysfunction is created. Parry's personal favorites include erectile dysfunction, adult attention deficit disorder, and premenstrual dysphoric disorder—a disorder so controversial some researchers say it doesn't even exist.

With rare candor Parry has explained how pharmaceutical companies now take the lead, not just in branding their blockbuster pills like Prozac and Viagra, but also in branding the conditions that create the markets for those pills. Working under the leadership of the drug marketers, Madison Avenue gurus like Parry get together with medical experts to "create new ideas about illnesses and conditions." The goal, he says, is to give drug company customers around the world "a new way to think about things." The aim, always, is to make the link between the condition and your medicine, in order to maximize its sales.

Drug Industry's Influence on Disease Definitions

The idea that drug companies help to create new illnesses may sound strange to many of us, but it is all too familiar to industry insiders. A recent *Reuters Business Insight* report designed for drug company executives argued that the ability to "create new disease markets" is bringing untold billions in soaring drug sales. One of the chief selling strategies, said the report, is to change the way people think about their common ailments, to make "natural processes" into medical conditions. People must be able to be "convinced" that "problems they may previously have accepted as, perhaps, merely an inconvenience"—like baldness, wrinkles, and sexual difficulties—are now seen as "worthy of medical intervention." Celebrating the development of profitable new disease markets like "Female Sexual Dysfunction," the report was upbeat about the financial future for the drug industry. "The coming years will bear greater witness to the corporate sponsored creation of disease."

The medical experts writing the rules [for diagnosing illness] are at the same time taking money from the drug makers who stand to make billions.

The unhealthy influence of the pharmaceutical industry has become a global scandal. That influence is fundamentally distorting medical science, corrupting the way medicine is practiced, and corroding the public's trust in their doctors. The burying of unfavorable research studies on children and antidepressants, the dangers of the anti-arthritis drugs and the investigations into the alleged bribing of physicians in Italy and the U.S. are just the latest in a string of embarrassments. Exploding drug expenditures have helped produce double-digit increases in the costs of health insurance premiums, fueling further widespread anger towards the industry, particularly in the U.S. As a result, many doctors, scientists, health advocates, politicians, and medical journal editors are moving to try to wind back the industry's influence over scientific research and doctors' prescribing habits. The time is ripe to understand how that influence now extends right to the very definitions of disease.

Marketing executives don't sit down and actually write the rules for how to diagnose illness, but they increasingly underwrite those who do. The industry now routinely sponsors key medical meetings where disease definitions are debated and updated. In some instances, as we will see, the medical experts writing the rules are at the same time taking money from the drug makers who stand to make billions, depending on how those rules are written. Many of the senior specialists deciding whether your sexual difficulties should be defined as sexual dysfunctions, whether your stomach complaints should be seen as serious medical conditions, and whether your everyday risks should be portrayed as deadly diseases, are on the payrolls of the companies seeking to sell you drugs. The payment of money doesn't necessarily buy influence, but in the eyes of many observers, doctors and drug companies have simply become too close.

Widening the Boundaries of Illness

With many medical conditions, there is great uncertainty about where to draw the line that separates, the healthy from the sick. The boundaries that separate "normal" and "abnormal" are often highly elastic, they may differ dramatically from country to country, and they can change over time. Clearly, the wider you draw the boundaries that define a disease, the wider the pool of potential patients, and the bigger the markets for those making drugs. The experts who sit down to draw those lines today are too often doing so with drug company pens in their hands, and they are drawing the boundaries wider and wider almost every time they meet.

According to these experts, 90 percent of the elderly in the U.S. will have a condition called high blood pressure, almost half of all women have a sexual dysfunction called FSD, and more than 40 million Americans should be taking drugs to lower their cholesterol. With a little help from a headline-hungry media, the latest condition is routinely portrayed as widespread, severe and, above all, treatable with drugs. Alternative ways of understanding or treating health problems, and lower estimates of the numbers affected, are often swept away by a frenzy of drug company promotion.

While the boundaries defining disease are pushed out as widely as they can be, by contrast, the causes of these supposed epidemics are portrayed as narrowly as possible. In the world of drug marketing, a major public health problem like heart disease can sometimes be reduced to a narrow focus on a person's cholesterol levels or blood pressure. Preventing hip fractures among the elderly becomes a narrow obsession with the bone density numbers of healthy middle-aged women. Personal distress is seen as being due largely to a chemical imbalance of serotonin in the brain, an explanation as narrow as it is outdated.

There are many different promotional strategies used in the selling of sickness, but the common factor among them all is the marketing of fear.

Like most everything else that happens in health care today, our ideas about sickness are being shaped in the long shadows cast by the global drug giants. Yet the narrowing of the focus is making it harder for us to see the bigger picture about health and disease, sometimes at great cost to the individual, and the community. To use a simple example, if an improvement in human health was our primary aim, some of the billions currently invested in expensive drugs to lower the cholesterol of the worried well might be far more efficiently spent on enhanced campaigns to reduce smoking, increase physical activity, and improve diet.

The Marketing of Fear

There are many different promotional strategies used in the selling of sickness, but the common factor among them all is the marketing of fear. The fear of heart attacks was used to sell women the idea that the menopause is a condition requiring hormone replacement. The fear of youth suicide is used to sell parents the idea that even mild depression must be treated with powerful drugs. The fear of an early death is used to sell high cholesterol as something automatically requiring a prescription. Yet ironically, the much-hyped medicines sometimes cause the very harm they are supposed to prevent.

Long-term hormone replacement therapy increases the risk of heart attacks for women, while antidepressants appear to increase the risk of suicidal thinking among the young. At least one of the blockbuster cholesterol-lowering drugs has been withdrawn from the market because it was implicated in *causing* deaths. In one of the most horrific cases of all, a drug sold as helping with common bowel problems led to constipation so severe for some people, they simply died. Yet in this case, as in so many others, the official government regulators somehow seemed more interested in protecting drug company profits than the public's health.

The pharmaceutical industry and its supporters defend their marketing campaigns as raising awareness about misunderstood diseases, and providing quality information about the latest medicines. Company executives talk of empowering consumers with advertising, and their paid celebrities are said to educate the public about health conditions via glossy magazine articles and on TV talk shows. Certainly there are some valuable examples of industry-sponsored efforts to destigmatize a health problem or stimulate much-needed action, as has occurred in the area of HIV-AIDS. Yet in other cases these campaigns are not education at all, but plain old promotion: skewing our understanding of the causes of human illness and distorting our knowledge of the remedies, playing up the benefits of drugs and playing down their harms and costs.

A loosening of advertising regulations in the late 1990s in the U.S. has delivered an unprecedented onslaught of drug marketing targeted at ordinary people, who now watch an average of ten or more of these advertisements every day. Likewise, viewers in New Zealand are subject to this sort of promotion. Elsewhere in the world the industry is fighting relentlessly for similar deregulation. For the supporters, this marketing is a valuable service; for the critics, it is putting disease at the center of human life. It is pushing the genuinely ill towards a limited range of the most expensive drug solutions, and making tens of millions of the healthy start to fear that their bodies are broken, dysfunctional, deficient, and decaying. This disease-mongering is an assault on our collective soul by those seeking to profit from our fear. It is no dark conspiracy, simply daylight robbery. . . .

Over three decades ago a maverick thinker called Ivan Illich raised alarms that an expanding medical establishment was "medicalizing" life itself, undermining the human capacity to cope with the reality of suffering and death, and making too many ordinary people into patients. He criticized a medical system "that claims authority over people who are not yet ill, people who cannot reasonably expect to get well, and those for whom doctors have no more effective treatment than that which could be offered by their uncles or aunts." A decade ago medical writer Lynn Payer described a process she called "disease-mongering": doctors and drug companies unnecessarily widening the boundaries of illness in order to see more patients and sell more drugs. In the years since, these writings have become ever more relevant, as the industry's marketing roar has grown louder and its grip on the health care system much stronger.

Soaring sales have made drug companies the most profitable corporations on the planet during particular years of the past decade. But the flip side of healthy returns for shareholders is an unsustainable increase in costs for those funding the health system, whether they are governments or private insurers. It is no surprise that the industry's unhealthy influence has become part of the political debate in many nations, which exploded in Australia during negotiations over the recent free trade deal with the U.S. As the public learns more about industry's influence over the definitions of disorders and dysfunctions, and its methods for creating "new disease markets" the selling of sickness will likely move closer to the center of those debates.

Drug Promotion Plays on People's Fears of Future Illness

Barbara Mintzes

Barbara Mintzes is a member of the faculty of the University of British Columbia Centre for Health Services and Policy Research.

Ray Moynihan [medical writer and coauthor of *Selling Sickness*] and colleagues describe disease mongering as, "widening the boundaries of treatable illness in order to expand markets for those who sell and deliver treatments." In this article, I examine one aspect of disease mongering: activities financed by drug companies to promote sales by expanding the pool of patients potentially treated by their products, when no benefit in terms of reduced morbidity [rate of illness] is likely. New diseases may be "created" or existing conditions redefined. In theory, these activities are covered by national laws governing drug promotion that forbid misleading or deceptive advertising. However, enforcement is piecemeal and largely ineffective. . . .

Full direct-to-consumer advertising (DTCA) of prescription drugs is legal in only the United States and New Zealand. However, in many other countries, unbranded disease-oriented advertising (in which no drug names are mentioned, but patients are often advised to "see your doctor") is increasingly common. . . .

A claimed benefit of disease-awareness campaigns is that the public becomes more aware of untreated health problems and seeks effective care at an earlier stage, leading to better health. For this to happen, the campaigns must address important health concerns, focus on patients likely to benefit

Barbara Mintzes, "Disease Mongering in Drug Promotion: Do Governments Have a Regulatory Role?" *PLoS Medicine*, April 11, 2006. Reproduced by permission.

from diagnosis and treatment, and steer them towards appropriate care. For the individual patient, drug treatment is worth pursuing if potential benefits outweigh potential harm. But as healthier people are targeted, the added benefit of drug treatment can become increasingly elusive.

Limited Regulatory Oversight

The US Food and Drug Administration (FDA) published a guidance in 2004 stating that unbranded adverts [ads] that are perceptually similar or otherwise linked to branded adverts are subject to FDA regulation, as are unbranded adverts by the manufacturer of the only drug in its class. Otherwise, the FDA has no authority over the content of disease-oriented advertising, although it recommends responsible public health messages. The United Kingdom Medicines Health-Care Products Regulatory Agency has issued guidelines stating that the primary purpose of disease-awareness advertising must be health education on a disease and its management, not product promotion. However, the Medicines Health-Care Products Regulatory Agency allowed Novartis' advertising on fungal nail infections (onychomycosis), which stressed high prevalence and infectiousness and guided viewers to prescription drugs, including Novartis' drug terbinafine (Lamisil).

Eight of the nine authors of the US cholesterol treatment guidelines released in 2004 had financial links to manufacturers.

In the Netherlands, a similar Novartis campaign for onychomycosis prompted the Dutch government to take Novartis to court for illegal DTCA. The government lost the case as neither the product nor the manufacturer was named. [Dutch researcher G.W.] 't Jong and colleagues subsequently analyzed the effects of the campaign on primary care, using administrative data covering 150 practices. They studied the changes in rates of prescriptions of oral terbinafine (Lamisil) and itraconazole (Sporanox, a competitor to Lamisil), and the onychomycosis consultation rate, before and after the start of the campaign. Both onychomycosis consultations and prescriptions for terbinafine (Lamisil) grew, whereas prescriptions for the competitor drug declined. Thus, an unbranded campaign had a brand-specific effect on sales, most likely because of concurrent branded promotion to physicians. 't Jong et al. noted the effects of promotion of a condition that is largely cosmetic (it usually causes no pain or suffering) on physicians' workload.

Promoting Sales Through Fear of Death

Pfizer, the manufacturer of Lipitor (atorvastatin), ran a campaign in France and Canada in 2003 with print adverts that used images of a tagged toe of a corpse.... On television, a youthful, healthy man died suddenly of a heart attack, leaving his family devastated with grief. The message of these two adverts was that cholesterol testing and treatment could prevent premature death from heart attacks in healthy people. This was at odds with existing scientific evidence: a 2003 meta-analysis of cholesterol-lowering drugs in primary prevention found no difference in mortality between drug and placebo.

Jonathan Quick and colleagues at the World Health Organization raised concerns in the *Lancet* that the adverts misinformed the public about cardiovascular risks and could lead to harm from medically unjustified drug use. They argued that governments should take a more active role in regulating disease-awareness campaigns to prevent misleading information from reaching the public. Complaints in Canada, which included the *Lancet* letter, resulted in no regulatory action. A subsequent advert shows a man walking down a city street, unaware that he is about to be charged by a rhinoceros. The tagline is the following: "Living with high cholesterol, you never know what's around the corner." The text stresses the risk of death from heart attacks. The only risk factor discussed is cholesterol.

Promotion of hormone replacement therapy (HRT) for disease prevention is a key example of disease mongering linked to drug sales.

Disease-awareness advertising is often the visible face of broader commercial influences. Eight of the nine authors of the US cholesterol treatment guidelines released in 2004 had financial links to manufacturers. . . . These guidelines extended treatment of high cholesterol to patient groups in which a morbidity and mortality advantage had not been established. A Pfizer financial report on atorvastatin (Lipitor) states, "There continues to be an opportunity for further growth of the cholesterol-lowering market. . . . Evolving treatment guidelines continue to encourage the broad use of statin therapy."

Hormone Replacement Therapy and Menopause

Promotion of hormone replacement therapy (HRT) for disease prevention is a key example of disease mongering linked to drug sales. Women learned to view menopause in terms of increased health risks that could be prevented with HRT. The first long-term randomized controlled trial of HRT in healthy women, the Women's Health Initiative, found a 1% increase in absolute risks for serious harm over five years, mainly due to cardiovascular adverse effects. The negative public health impact of HRT use by millions of women worldwide is likely to have been considerable. Regulatory agencies have changed labelling to warn potential users of serious risks and to advise limiting use to short-term symptomatic treatment, but have taken no broader action to review marketing of drugs for disease prevention.

On 28 December 2005, the first hit on a Google search on "menopause and estrogen deficiency" was a Merck Web site promoting an estrogen patch, and linking postmenopausal estrogen deficiency to reduced performance, fine motor skills, memory, and a reduction in "planned, targeted, flexible and adaptable thought."

In 2006, a handbook for journalists, called *The Journalist's Menopause Handbook*, which was funded by Wyeth Canada and produced by a medical society (the Society of Obstetricians and Gynaecologists of Canada), fails to mention increased risks of strokes, heart attacks, pulmonary emboli, or symptoms of probable dementia associated with HRT. The magnitude of breast cancer risk is described as no greater than lifestyle-associated risks. Hot flushes, mood and memory, appearance (wrinkles), sleep disturbances, bladder control, and sexual changes are listed as menopausal symptoms. Short-term HRT for moderate to severe symptoms is recommended as safe and effective, with "short-term" defined as up to five years. Beyond the lack of established link between wrinkles and menopause (rather than ageing per se), is HRT really a reasonable treatment for wrinkles, given the cardiovascular, cancer, and dementia risks?

Lower Thresholds for Symptomatic Treatment

[Researcher M.] Mamdani and colleagues found that following the launch of celecoxib (Celebrex) and rofecoxib (Vioxx), more elderly patients in Ontario were treated with nonsteroidal anti-inflammatory drugs (NSAIDs) than previously. The increase was attributable to use of Cox-2 inhibitors by people not previously taking NSAIDs. Paradoxically, although these newer drugs were promoted for greater gastrointestinal safety, Mamdani and colleagues found that approximately 650 more hospitalizations for gastrointestinal bleeds occurred per year after the drugs' introduction. In their conclusion, the authors stated the following: "Although we cannot prove causation, we believe that the striking temporal correlation, biological plausibility, and lack of any other trends that would explain the association strongly suggest that the two events are directly related."

Another heavily promoted class of drugs are the proton pump inhibitors. [Researcher J.] Bashford and colleagues analyzed why patients were prescribed proton pump inhibitors during a five-year period in which prescribing increased 10-fold. By 1995, 46% of prescriptions were for off-label uses, mainly milder problems. In 2004, researchers found a link between use of proton pump inhibitors and higher risks of *Clostridium difficile* [an intestinal bug] infection in hospitalized patients. A US magazine advertisement for esomeprazole (Nexium) in November 2005 (e.g., printed in *Family Circle*), a year after this study, warns readers that "something could be brewing" beneath their heartburn. A distressed woman is shown with a red scarf around her neck, and on the scarf is the following statement: "Behind this scarf acid could be burning the lining of her esophagus." The advert quotes a high rate of erosive esophagitis among people with acid reflux, one in three, based on data on file at AstraZeneca. Although the advert contains the disclaimer that "only a doctor can determine if you have this condition," the image of distress and the larger headlines—such as "Acid reflux disease can damage your esophagus" and "Nexium heals the damage"—convey the message to be anxious about heartburn and consider it a possible sign of more serious disease. Like many US adverts, this one offers a free trial. . . .

A Mixed Regulatory Response

Unlike many countries that rely primarily on industry self-regulation, the FDA regulates prescription drug promotion directly. Letters of violation to manufacturers are posted on the FDA Web site. . . . For 15 out of 21 (71%) letters, reviewers from the FDA's Division of Drug Marketing, Advertising, and Communications raised concerns related to disease mongering. These concerns often consisted of (1) off-label promotion broadening approved indications and (2) misrepresentation of disease so as to exaggerate treatment effectiveness.

Many examples also exist of disease mongering in US DTCA that has not been subject to regulation. In a recent article in *PLoS Medicine*, [J.] Lacasse and [J.] Leo reviewed the evidence supporting the hypothesis that depression is caused by a serotonin deficiency, concluding that a lack of evidence exists to support this hypothesis. They questioned the FDA's lack of attention to the claims in SSRI adverts for antidepressants that depression and anxiety disorders are caused by a chemical imbalance in the brain. . . .

Disease mongering by definition creates erroneous impressions of the condition a product aims to treat and the merit and safety of treatment, and frequently provokes undue anxiety.

[Researcher Edward] Kravitz and colleagues found more broadly that patient requests for advertised medicines could lead to off-label antidepressant prescribing for "adjustment disorder," a disorder involving temporary distress due to a troubling life situation that rarely requires drug treatment. Standardized patients received antidepressant prescriptions just over half the time if they requested the advertised antidepressant Paxil, whether they had symptoms of depression or adjustment disorder. If patients had not requested a drug, physicians were much less likely to prescribe antidepressants for adjustment disorder. This study provides experimental evidence of a link bet-000ween patient requests for medicines and unnecessary medicalization. . . .

Is More Regulation Needed?

The rationale for regulation of drug promotion is health protection, encouragement of appropriate medicine use, and prevention of deceptive advertising. . . .

The World Health Organization's Ethical Criteria for Medicinal Drug Promotion states that advertisements, ". . .should not take undue advantage of people's concern for their health."

Disease mongering by definition creates erroneous impressions of the condition a product aims to treat and the merit and safety of treatment, and frequently provokes undue anxiety or exaggerates prevalence rates.

The prohibition of DTCA is consistent with regulatory aims to protect health and encourage appropriate medicine use. Unbranded disease-awareness campaigns for the condition a manufacturer's drug aims to treat are a form of DTCA. If these adverts are allowed under laws guaranteeing commercial freedom of expression, a regulatory rationale remains to (1) de-link them from suggestions to "ask your doctor" for a treatment and (2) to insist on prescreening of adverts by a government agency to ensure conformity with the law before they are broadcast or printed. Similarly, drug company funding of media promotions aiming to stimulate sales should be subject to the same regulatory control as direct advertising.

The public can expect more unfettered disease mongering warning them that without the latest treatment, life will be grim indeed.

Better definitions are needed of the indications drugs are approved to treat to ensure consistency with assessed outcomes in premarket trials. Evidence of benefit should be based on clinical outcomes, and greater caution is needed in introducing new diagnoses.

A key question is whether there is sufficient political will among government regulatory agencies to better enforce existing regulations governing drug promotion or to introduce new solutions. Most regulatory agencies fail to treat regulation of drug promotion as a public health concern. Unless this changes, the public can expect more unfettered disease mongering warning them that without the latest treatment, life will be grim indeed.

Drug Promotion Has Led to the Overmedication of Children

Anne Taylor Fleming

Anne Taylor Fleming is a nationally recognized journalist and on-camera essayist for The NewsHour with Jim Lehrer. *She is also the author of several books.*

I'm not sure when I became aware of how pervasive drug use has become among the people around me.

I'm talking completely legal drug use, not just by the adults but by their children. Walk through any school at any grade level anywhere in this country and you can bet there are students routinely taking Ritalin or Adderall for attention-deficit/hyperactivity disorder, Prozac or Paxil or Zoloft for depression.

It's astonishing to think how pervasively these drugs have taken hold, how quickly we went from pot to Prozac, from a nation aghast at the use of drugs in the '80s to a nation encouraging their use 20 years later, even for the very young.

In 2002, 11 million prescriptions for antidepressants were written for our kids. Do we really believe that around one out of every seven children belong on drugs?

FDA-mandated warning labels [are] just a speed bump on the highway to the increasingly pharmacological future.

We have just had our first sharp warning sign that we've been too quick to medicate. Some pharmaceutical companies actually tried to suppress the warning signs, specifically the

Anne Taylor Fleming, "Drug Fix," *NewsHour with Jim Lehrer*, November 26, 2004. www.pbs.org/newshour. Reproduced by permission.

fact that antidepressants can actually increase suicidal thoughts and tendencies in kids who take them.

Now those pills will come with FDA-mandated warning labels not unlike the little black boxes on cigarette packages. My guess is that it's just a speed bump on the highway to the increasingly pharmacological future.

There's too much money in it, too many companies, and, let's be honest, plenty of adults who were enamored of mood-altering drugs when they were kids.

And there's also an emphasis on brain science now, on research showing that our emotions and fears are all neuro-chemically driven. Why not calm an erratic wild child with a daily dose of Ritalin? Isn't that kinder than letting him or her flail through the formative years?

Why not buoy an unhappy teen with antidepressants? Isn't that more efficient than a combination of talk therapy and exercise and maybe a healthy diet? That's one side of the argument.

But there's another side, the perhaps retro notion that we are more than our synapses and that we should learn to live with our sorrows and griefs and ragged loves and losses, not treat them as afflictions, and that if we medicate our kids, they will not learn to manage their own moods and behavior.

There is a sense, too, that harried parents too often accede to the use of these drugs because they don't have the time or energy for their children, and that school administrators too quickly urge the use of drugs to resolve behavioral or developmental problems that they don't have the resources or expertise to deal with.

This is not to argue against using drugs for the disturbed, in tandem preferably with good, old-fashioned talking therapy. But it is to question if we as a culture are throwing drugs at everything, every mood twitch and disappointment and emotional trauma because it is easier than dealing with the problem.

At the bottom of all this is the strange feeling that we are farther down a chemical road than we even imagined. Part of it is the drug companies, but only part of it. The other part is this is who many of us are now.

This is how we think of ourselves and our loved ones, as people whose souls and psyches can be fixed if we can only find the right pill.

Drugs for Minor Conditions Are Important to Many People

Glenn Harlan Reynolds

Glenn Harlan Reynolds is a law professor at the University of Tennessee, the creator of the widely read blog InstaPundit, a contributor to many major publications, and the author of several books.

Though the subject has receded from the forefront of public debate for the moment, prescription drug prices remain a likely political issue. . . . I'm not entirely sure what to do about it, although I strongly suspect that the usual redistributionist, "soak the evil corporations" nostrums would—as always—prove utterly disastrous if enacted. I also think that it will be difficult . . . to resist those pressures, given that senior citizens are among the Democratic Party's remaining core constituencies, and given that senior citizens have little incentive to support policies that will produce better drugs in the future at the cost of higher drug prices now. They're around now to reap the benefit of lower drug prices, and if they cared about their grandkids, well, they wouldn't be so resistant to Social Security reform, would they?. . .

But I want to respond to something different. I hear a lot of complaint from people who object to the pharmaceutical industry's work on what are often described as frivolous products, like Viagra or drugs for treating acid reflux disease. I'm not sure that these drugs account for a major part of prescription drug costs—among the best selling drugs most are for treating heart disease or mental illness—but I do wonder just how frivolous such matters are. The term "dyspeptic," after all, describes an irritable disposition arising from stomach pain. As somebody who suffers from reflux myself, I can attest that acid-lowering drugs like aciphex and prilosec are lifesavers.

In terms of quality of life, they're certainly that. (In terms of reduced risk of stomach and esophageal cancer, they may be lifesavers down the line as well, with concomitant savings in medical costs). What's the dollar value of a life spent without stabbing pains in one's midsection? I don't know, but most people who take acid-lowering drugs consider the relief cheap at the price.

I hope that the [pharmaceutical price] debaters will . . . not engage in elitist talk about which problems are worthy of solution, and which are not.

Viagra seems more frivolous, though I'm not sure why. My grandfather, suffering from impotence because of heart problems, submitted to coronary bypass surgery when it was still very new and risky. The surgery was expensive, and he wound up dying from complications. He knew the risk, but preferred to take the chance rather than live with impotence. My father has remarked that if Viagra had been invented then, his father might have lived considerably longer.

Was he silly to feel that way? Some people might say so, of course. But whether you think that his choice was one you might make, it's a clear indicator of just how important the benefits that drugs like Viagra bring are to some people. Not frivolous.

Likewise, although drugs that relieve depression are viewed by some as being frivolous—standing in the path of the "authentic" existence that intellectuals always seem to define in terms of sadness rather than joy—they are quite literally lifesavers for some people who might otherwise commit suicide.

And even for those who wouldn't, they're an alternative to a life of misery. If you're pro-misery, I guess that's bad, but I'm not.

So as the debate goes on regarding pharmaceutical prices, I hope that the debaters will keep their eye on the ball—how to promote progress in producing new drugs that solve long-standing problems—and not engage in elitist talk about which problems are worthy of solution, and which are not. A cure for cancer may take longer than a cure for heartburn, but both are cures—which is more than the drug-price critics have managed to come up with.

Improved Prescription Drugs Mean Better Medical Treatment and Less Illness

Alan F. Holmer

Alan F. Holmer was the president of the Pharmaceutical Research and Manufacturers of America (PhRMA) at the time he made this speech to its members. In February 2007 he was appointed Special Envoy for China and the Strategic Economic Dialogue (SED) at the U.S. Treasury Department.

Our association's strength comes from what our companies do every day. From the knowledge, creativity and gritty perseverance of our people. It begins in our great corporate enterprises and legions of individual lives dedicated to advance and apply science to help and heal.

The new medicines that your companies invent save lives—from the premature baby whose lungs are not yet well enough formed to breathe, to the elderly lymphoma patient whose cancer is put into remission, allowing her to see the day her first great-grandchild is born.

And the new medicines that your companies invent add immeasurably to quality of life. From the patient with schizophrenia who is able to lead a productive and good life with his family rather than being confined to a mental hospital, to the patient with heart disease who is able to lead the active retirement she had imagined, rather than a life tethered to an oxygen tank.

Our industry's commitment to humane values is also expressed through our patient assistance programs that bring free medicines to millions of uninsured or under-insured pa-

Alan F. Holmer, "The Cycle of Hope: Breaking the Cycle of Doom," March 28, 2003. Reproduced by permission of International Federation of Pharmaceutical Manufacturers & Associations from http://www.ifpma.org/News/SpeechDetail.aspx?nID=495.

tients, our unparalleled philanthropy, our efforts in partnerships to help build needed health care infrastructure in less developed countries, and much, much more.

Doomsayers assert that drug costs are rising because pharmaceutical companies are getting doctors to prescribe—and patients to take—new, more costly medicines they don't need.

Like all others who engage in commerce, we are in business and businesses need to make money. Our businesses make money in a way that alleviates pain and suffering, increases productivity, advances human knowledge, and invests in a better future. . . .

Public Policy Debate

Notwithstanding our successes as an industry and an association, everyone in this room knows the magnitude of the challenges we face in the public policy arena. Underlying all of these challenges is a public policy debate about medicines based on inadequate, misleading, and sometimes simply false information. Today, much of it is framed by what one PhRMA Board member has labeled "the cycle of doom."

The "cycle of doom" starts with the claim that rapidly increasing drug costs are making health care unaffordable, bankrupting America, and ruining the competitiveness of American businesses. Doomsayers assert that drug costs are rising because pharmaceutical companies are getting doctors to prescribe and patients to take—new, more costly medicines they don't need. And that because of this pharmaceutical marketing, "drug costs are going up 20% per year"—our critics say that like It's one word—"drugcostsaregoingup20%peryear"—and so the cycle continues.

As an industry, our task is to replace "the cycle of doom" with "the cycle of hope."

The "cycle of hope" starts with the recognition that as medicines improve and increasingly treat underlying diseases and not just symptoms, medical care improves with greater use of such medicines. With these changes, more Americans are getting earlier and better treatments for diseases that once consigned them to an invariable downward spiral of disability or even death. The benefits grow as we tell doctors and patients—including millions of previously untreated or under-treated patients—about new medicines, allowing patients to avoid or reduce hospitalizations, lost time at work, and suffering. The cycle of hope continues as part of the return on investment in each medicine is plowed back into research, giving us the opportunity to make more progress against disease, more improvements to health care and new possibilities for patients.

The cycle of hope means that medicines are a growing share of the health care dollar. The alternative is stagnation. For instance, spending on medicines would be lower without the Alzheimer's drugs that delay nursing home admissions. But then we'd spend far more on nursing homes. Not a good trade. And when we invent the even better Alzheimer's medicines that we need, spending on drugs will go up some more. That's a big problem if you believe in the cycle of doom. It's exactly what should happen if you believe in the cycle of hope. . . .

Let's examine the cycle of doom through a simple analogy.

Suppose I argued that the cost of information technology threatens to bankrupt America and destroy America's competitiveness in the world economy. To support this claim, I could refer you to the near-geometric increase in the amount Americans—private individuals, employers, and governments—are spending on computer technology. In 1950, total U.S. expenditures for computer technology and software were close to zero. In 2002, U.S. businesses and other consumers spent about $430 billion on IT [information technologies].

And the requirement for computers for students and on college campuses has increased the costs of education.

Ohmygosh! Thecostofcomputershasgoneup$430billion!!

And, because the information technology industry is so innovative, the state of the art is constantly advancing. That means that people want newer, better products all the time—particularly in view of the IT industry's aggressive marketing. By the end of the decade [2010], this runaway spending—which is increasing at double-digit rates—could exceed one trillion dollars!

And suppose I told you that to avoid this economic Armageddon, we should adopt a national policy to undermine the information technology industry's intellectual property protection, restrict access to computers, prohibit IT companies from advertising, and do everything else we can to discourage future innovation in this industry.

I suspect that you'd shake your head in disbelief at these claims. Yet these are precisely the arguments made about medicines.

It's time for us to challenge these claims with the same knowledge, creativity and perseverance that we, as an industry, bring every day to discovering new and better medicines.

Rising Drug Costs

Having established that context, let's look at the often-heard claims that drug costs are unsustainable and making health care unaffordable.

If you only read the headlines and listened to the debate in Congress, you would get the impression that prescription drugs are single-handedly responsible for increasing health care costs. This is a little like blaming increasing book expenditures for the rising cost of college tuition. In fact, according to the latest government study, outpatient prescription medicines accounted for only 9.9 percent of total health care costs in 2001.

One dime out of every health care dollar for all of our medicines. And that dime includes not only innovative brand-name medicines, but also the cost of generic drugs, PBM [pharmacy benefit managers] and pharmacy costs, and all other costs in the pharmaceutical distribution chain.

Something as valuable as medicines that change the course of disease while accounting for about one-tenth of the total cost of health care shouldn't cause such a disproportionate amount of hand-wringing. . . .

There are a number of broken axles in our health care system; the modern miracle of pharmaceuticals isn't one of them.

So I come back to the one word we hear in so many political forums, "Drugcostsgoingup20%peryear." Of course, this past year [2002], the increase was really 11.8%. And of that, fully 8 percentage points were not for price increases, but rather for increasing use of medicines by patients and the shift from older, less effective medicines to newer, more effective medicines.

Some look at the increasing use of medicines and the shift to newer medicines as problems to be solved, not solutions for patients and contributions to affordable health care. They don't want to acknowledge the data showing that even well-insured patients under-use asthma medicines and antidepressants. They don't want to focus on the need for more use of medicines to treat heart disease, hypertension and other conditions. These are facts that we need to drive into policy debates. There are a number of broken axles in our health care system; the modern miracle of pharmaceuticals isn't one of them.

Let's look at another condition—diabetes. In the last decade, spending on medicines to treat diabetes skyrocketed from $1.3 billion to $7.3 billion. That's a 455% increase in one decade. Over three-quarters of this increase went to newer oral diabetes medicines. All of this is very alarming if you believe in the cycle of doom. Our critics would say, "We can't possibly afford a 455% increase in spending on diabetes medicines. And surely we're wasting enormous sums of money on those new medicines."

Those who look at the facts will see at work the cycle of hope, rather than the cycle of doom. Spending has increased in part because the number of patients diagnosed with diabetes increased by almost half over the past decade. So we're treating far more patients. We're treating them earlier and more aggressively, since we now know that keeping blood glucose levels lower and more tightly controlled slows or avoids the progression of this disease's terrible complications. And as we gain better understanding of diabetes, we've brought five new classes of medicines to patients since 1995. These medicines greatly expand treatment options, allowing physicians to better tailor treatment to individual patients' needs, sometimes using combination therapy, and to reduce or avoid side effects. And increased spending on medicines for diabetes patients can help achieve overall savings on their health costs and avoid hospitalizations.

Working Toward a Cure

The cycle of hope continues in your companies' research laboratories, as we work toward a cure for diabetes. Today, there are many new pharmaceutical treatments in development, ranging from inhaled forms of insulin that would not require injections; to compounds that modify the metabolism of fat cells; to proteins that promote increased insulin production when blood sugar levels are high, but not when they are normal; and much more.

I know that diabetes treatment is part of the cycle of hope. To those who perpetuate the cycle of doom and say we can't afford today's medicines, I ask:

- Which of the five new classes of diabetes medicines brought to patients since 1995 would you choose to forego?

- Would you propose that we abandon the new standards of care so that we can spend less on diabetes medicines?—standards of care that emphasize earlier treatment and tighter control of blood sugar levels.

- Which of the new treatments being researched and developed today should we take out of the pipeline for under-treated diabetes patients?

- And, are you prepared to pay more for other health care services in order to cut the ten cents of the health care dollar that we spend on drugs?

Today, few policymakers know the facts I've outlined—all they hear is that drug costs are unsustainable, that drug costs are going up 20% per year. We need to give them the facts about diabetes, and similar facts about all the other conditions that can be treated more effectively because of new medicines. And we must broaden the focus of discussion from health care to health itself, facing up to the consequences of choices and lifestyles, while thanking heaven for the ingenuity and persistence of the American pharmaceutical industry.

It makes no sense for our companies to discover and develop new medicines if doctors and patients don't know they exist.

In sum, our job is to challenge those who define increased use of needed medicines and increased spending on medicines as problems rather than solutions. If they believe that increased use of new and better medicines is a problem, then we should ask them to provide their vision of patient care, and to explain how it is superior to ours, in patient terms as well as economic terms. If conducted honestly and fully, I'm confident about how that debate would turn out.

Some critics have their own favored explanation for why use of medicines is increasing. They don't want to focus on increasing prevalence of disease, broader treatment options as medicines improve, and evidence-based standards of medical care that emphasize earlier and more use of medicines. Rather, their explanation is that increased use of medicines is purely a result of direct-to-consumer advertising and other types of promotion, topics to which I'll now turn.

Marketing and Consumer Health Information

It makes no sense for our companies to discover and develop new medicines if doctors and patients don't know they exist. That's why we work to inform doctors about treatment options. [Former PhRMA board chairman] Fred Hassan described in his remarks our adoption [in 2002] of a new PhRMA Code for Interactions with Health Care Professionals, to ensure that company efforts are education- and patient-centered.

We also share information about our products directly to consumers. Consumer health information on pharmaceuticals has brought millions of patients into needed medical care, according to research by the FDA and others. It also enhances patients' compliance with physician-directed treatment. Despite these proven successes, our advertising is often criticized in the U.S. And it's just plain forbidden in Europe, where government-run health systems have adopted a policy of "don't tell, don't ask:" Don't tell patients about innovative medicines and they hope that patients don't ask. . . .

We fight for consumer health information so that all patients can get the best medicines their doctor prescribes for them with their unique medical needs. It's time for us to stop just defending promotion, and to start calling on its critics to explain their opposition. For example, the critics should explain either that they prefer that millions of patients remain untreated, or just what is their different and better way for helping them, I'll bet their alternative has three hallmarks: more government, restricted information and little patient choice.

I'm confident that when the truth is presented and understood, we will prevail. Because America is a cycle of hope kind of country. Our job is to explain these contending visions to decision-makers in unambiguous terms. So that they understand the cycle of hope and start asking the right questions about the cycle of doom. . . .

My sweet, gentle, 83-year-old mother was prescribed a medicine for high blood pressure. The medicine worked, but the side effects made her dizzy and made her face swell. Fortunately, she was able to switch to another drug, which treated her problem effectively with no noticeable side effects. I am sure that some of our critics would have called that a "me too" drug.

But what if my Mom hadn't been able to switch? What if she had been in a top-down, government-run program with a one-drug-fits-all policy?

We need to let patients and doctors—not government officials—make choices about the best medicines for each individual patient. Seniors and the disabled should have access to the best, most innovative medicines we can invent, and the medicines their doctors believe would work best for them.

A Choice Between Life and Death

I want to leave you with one more individual tale. It has to do with a relatively rare but devastating disease called chronic myeloid leukemia. One of our companies—Novartis—spent hundreds of millions of dollars to come up with a breakthrough drug to fight it.

In the heat and hassle of travel [in] August [2002], the son of one of the 20,000 patients with this disease happened to be sitting on an airplane next to a Novartis employee. She was going about her business, reviewing some materials, and the man noticed the company logo.

"I hope you don't mind," he said, "but I want to tell you a story. About two years ago, my father was diagnosed with chronic myeloid leukemia. Shortly after that, one of your drugs, Gleevec, was approved for testing. My father was made part of this test group. The drug saved his life. If it wasn't for Gleevec, we wouldn't have him with us today."

"You know," he said, "You hear so many negative things about drug companies. . . ."

The woman from Novartis was gracious in response. But we must make it clear to policy makers that his father lives because Novartis, like the rest of our companies, is free to discover and manufacture—and, yes, promote—miracles. That's why we go to work every day. That's why our work is both more challenging and more rewarding than simply being in business. It's about the cycle of hope.

It's been said that motives and purposes are in the brain and heart of man. Consequences are in the world of fact. We, at PhRMA, will continue to do our best to explain the nobility of our companies' intentions and the poetry of our people's science. But I promise you this: we will insist on debate based on truth and facts. We will force admission that the choice is literally between life and death; between the possibilities of choice and hope or restrictions and doom.

We choose life. We are the engines of the cycle of hope, and we will not fail.

Direct-to-Consumer Prescription Drug Advertising Helps People Get Treatment for Undiagnosed Diseases

Paul Antony

Paul Antony is the chief medical officer for the Pharmaceutical Research and Manufacturers of America (PhRMA).

Surveys indicate that DTC [direct-to-consumer] advertising makes consumers aware of new drugs and their benefits, as well as risks and side effects with the drugs advertised. They help consumers recognize symptoms and seek appropriate care. According to an article in the *New England Journal of Medicine*, DTC advertising is concentrated among a few therapeutic categories. These are therapeutic categories in which consumers can recognize their own symptoms, such as arthritis, seasonal allergies, and obesity; or for pharmaceuticals that treat chronic diseases with many undiagnosed sufferers, such as high cholesterol, osteoporosis, and depression.

DTC advertising gets patients talking to their doctors about conditions that may otherwise have gone undiagnosed or undertreated. For example, a study conducted by RAND Health and published in the *New England Journal of Medicine* found that nearly half of all adults in the United States fail to receive recommended health care. According to researchers on the RAND study, "the deficiencies in care . . . pose serious threats to the health of the American public that could contribute to thousands of preventable deaths in the United States each year." The study found underuse of prescription medications in seven of the nine conditions for which prescription medicines were the recommended treatment. Conditions for which

Paul Antony, testimony before the U.S. Senate Special Committee on Aging, www.ph rma.org, September 29, 2005. Reproduced by permission.

underuse was found include asthma, cerebrovascular disease, congestive heart failure [CHF], diabetes, hip fracture, hyperlipidemia and hypertension. Of those seven conditions for which RAND found underuse of recommended prescription medicines, five are DTC advertised.

The RAND Study, as well as other studies, highlight the underuse of needed medications and other healthcare services in the U.S.

- According to a nationally representative study of 9,090 people aged 18 and up, published in *JAMA* [*Journal of the American Medical Association*], about 43 percent of participants with recent major depression are getting inadequate therapy.

- A 2004 study published in the *Archives of Internal Medicine*, found that, "in older patients, failures to prescribe indicated medications, monitor medications appropriately, document necessary information, educate patients, and maintain continuity are more common prescribing problems than is use of inappropriate drugs."

- A May/June 2003 study published in the *Journal of Managed Care Pharmacy*, which examined claims data from 3 of the 10 largest health plans in California to determine the appropriateness of prescription medication use based upon widely accepted treatment guidelines, found that "effective medication appears to be underused." Of the four therapeutic areas of study— asthma, CHF, depression, and common cold or upper respiratory tract infections—asthma, CHF, and depression were undertreated. The researchers concluded that "the results are particularly surprising and disturbing when we take into account the fact that three of the conditions studied (asthma, CHF, and depression) are known to produce high costs to the healthcare system."

- According to a study released in May 2005 by the Stanford University School of Medicine, among patients with high cholesterol in moderate and high-risk groups, researchers found fewer than half of patient visits ended with a statin recommendation. Based on the findings, the researchers say physicians should be more aggressive in investigating statin therapy for patients with a high or moderate risk of heart disease, and that patients should ask for their cholesterol levels to be checked regularly.

Increasing Doctor-Patient Communication

A vast majority of patients (93 percent) who asked about a drug reported that their doctor "welcomed the questions." Of patients who asked about a drug, 77 percent reported that their relationship with their doctor remained unchanged as a result of the office visit, and 20 percent reported that their relationship improved. In addition, both an FDA [Food and Drug Administration] survey of physicians (from a random sample of 500 physicians from the American Medical Association's database) and a survey by the nation's oldest and largest African-American medical association, found that DTC advertisements raise disease awareness and bolster doctor-patient ties.

The doctor-patient relationship is enhanced if DTC advertising prompts a patient to talk to his doctor for the first time about a previously undiscussed condition, to comply with a prescribed treatment regimen, or to become aware of a risk or side effect that was otherwise unknown. A 2002 *Prevention* magazine survey found that 24.8 million Americans spoke with their doctor about a medical condition for the first time as a result of seeing a DTC advertisement. Similarly, the FDA patient survey on DTC advertising found that nearly one in five patients reported speaking to a physician about a condition for the first time because of a DTC ad.

PhRMA and its member companies believe it is vital that patients, in consultation with their doctors, make decisions about treatments and medicines. Prescribing decisions should be dominated by the doctor's advice. While our member companies direct a large majority of their promotional activities toward physicians, such promotion in no way guarantees medicines will be prescribed.

According to reports and studies, there is no direct relationship between DTC advertising and the price growth of drugs.

According to a General Accounting [now "Accountability"] Office report, of the 61.1 million people (33 percent of adults) who had discussions with their physician as a result of a DTC advertisement in 2001, only 8.5 million (5 percent of adults) actually received a prescription for the product, a small percentage of the total volume of prescriptions dispensed. Indeed, an FDA survey of physicians revealed that the vast majority of physicians do not feel pressure to prescribe. According to the survey, 91 percent of physicians said that their patients did not try to influence treatment courses in a way that would have been harmful and 72 percent of physicians, when asked for prescription for a specific brand name drug, felt little or no pressure to prescribe a medicine.

Destigmatizing Disease

DTC advertising also encourages patients to discuss medical problems that otherwise may not have been discussed because it was either thought to be too personal or that there was a stigma attached to the disease. For example, a *Health Affairs* article examined the value of innovation and noted that depression medications, known as selective serotonin reuptake inhibitors (SSRIs), that have been DTC advertised, have led to significant treatment expansion. Prior to the 1990's, it was estimated that about half of those persons who met a clinical definition of depression were not appropriately diagnosed, and many of those diagnosed did not receive clinically appropriate treatment. However, in the 1990's with the advent of SSRIs, treatment has been expanded. According to the article, "Manufacturers of SSRIs encouraged doctors to watch for depression, and the reduced stigma afforded by the new medications induced patients to seek help." As a result, diagnosis and treatment for depression doubled over the 1990's.

Utilization and DTC Advertising

According to reports and studies, there is no direct relationship between DTC advertising and the price growth of drugs. For example, in comments to the FDA in December 2003, the FTC [Federal Trade Commission] stated, "[DTC advertising] can empower consumers to manage their own health care by providing information that will help them, with the assistance of their doctors, to make better informed decisions about their treatment options. ... Consumers receive these benefits from DTC advertising with little, if any, evidence that such advertising increases prescription drug prices." Notably, since January 2000, the CPI [Consumer Price Index] component that tracks prescription medicines have been in line with overall medical inflation.

The FTC comments referenced above also note, "DTC advertising accounts for a relatively small proportion of the total cost of drugs, which reinforces the view that such advertising would have a limited, if any, effect on price." ...

One study in the *American Journal of Managed Care* looked at whether pharmaceutical marketing has led to an increase in the use of medications by patients with marginal indications. The study found that high-risk individuals were receiving lipid-lowering treatment "consistent with evidence-based practice guidelines" despite the fact that "a substantial portion of patients continue to remain untreated and undertreated. ..."

The study concluded that "greater overall use did not appear to be associated with a shift towards patients with less CV [cardiovascular] risk."

Many new medicines replace higher-cost surgeries and hospital care.

Pharmaceutical utilization is increasing for reasons other than DTC advertising. As the June 2003 study of DTC advertising commissioned by the Kaiser Family Foundation found, "[Our] estimates indicate that DTCA is important, but not the primary driver of recent growth [in prescription drug spending]."

Other reasons pharmaceutical utilization is increasing, include:

- *Improved Medicines*—Many new medicines replace higher-cost surgeries and hospital care. In 2004 alone, pharmaceutical companies added 38 new medicines and over the last decade, over 300 new medicines have become available for treating patients. These include important new medicines for some of the most devastating and costly diseases, including: AIDS, cancer, heart disease, Alzheimer's, and diabetes. According to a study prepared for the Department of Health and Human Services, "[n]ew medications are not simply more costly than older ones. They may be more effective or have fewer side effects; some may treat conditions for which no treatment was available."

- *New Standards of Medical Practice Encouraging Greater Use of Pharmaceuticals*—Clinical standards are changing to emphasize earlier and tighter control of a range of conditions, such as diabetes, hypertension and cardiovascular disease. For example, new recommendations from the two provider groups suggest that early treatment, including lifestyle changes and treatment with two or more types of medications, can significantly reduce the risk of later complications and improve the quality of life for people with type 2 diabetes.

- *Greater Treatment of Previously Undiagnosed and Untreated Conditions*—According to guidelines developed by the National Heart, Lung, and Blood Institute's National Cholesterol Education Program (NCEP) Adult Treatment Panel (ATP), approximately 36 million adults should be taking medicines to lower their cholesterol, a number that has grown from 13 million just 8 years ago [in 1997].

- *Aging of America*—The aging of America translates into greater reliance on pharmaceuticals. For example, congestive heart failure affects an estimated 2 percent of Americans aged 40 to 59, more than 5 percent of those aged 60 to 69, and 10 percent of those 70 or more.

While some assume that DTC advertising leads to increased use of newer medicines rather than generic medicines, generics represent just over 50 percent of all prescriptions (generics are historically not DTC advertised). In contrast, in Europe, where DTC advertising is prohibited, the percentage of prescriptions that are generic is significantly lower. Likewise, it is worth noting that while broadcast DTC has been in place since 1997, the rate of growth in drug cost increases has declined in each of the last 5 years [2000–2004] and in 2004 was below the rate of growth in overall health care costs.

Economic Value of DTC Advertising

Increased spending on pharmaceuticals often leads to lower spending on other forms of more costly health care. New drugs are the most heavily advertised drugs, a point critics often emphasize. However, the use of newer drugs tends to lower all types of non-drug medical spending, resulting in a net reduction in the total cost of treating a condition. For example, on average, replacing an older drug with a drug 15 years newer increases spending on drugs by $18, but reduces overall costs by $111.

The Tufts Center for the Study of Drug Development reports that disease management organizations surveyed believe that increased spending on prescription drugs reduces hospital inpatient costs. "Since prescription drugs account for less than 10 percent of total current U.S. health care spending, while inpatient care accounts for 32 percent, the increased use of appropriate pharmaceutical therapies may help moderate or reduce growth in the costliest component of the U.S. health care system," according to Tufts Center Director Kenneth I. Kaitin.

DTC advertising provides value to patients by making them aware of risks and benefits of new drugs.

Opponents also compare the amount of money spent by drug companies on marketing and advertising to the amount they spend on research and development [R&D] of new drugs. However, in 2004, pharmaceutical manufacturers spent an estimated $4.15 billion on DTC advertising, according to [pharmaceutical marketing intelligence firm] IMS Health, compared to $49.3 billion in total R&D spending by the biopharmaceutical industry, according to [life sciences consultants] Burrill & Company. PhRMA members alone spent $38.8 billion on R&D in 2004.

DTC advertising provides value to patients by making them aware of risks and benefits of new drugs; it empowers patients and enhances the public health; it plays a vital role in addressing a major problem in this country of undertreatment and underdiagnosis of disease; encourages patients to discuss medical problems with their health care provider that may otherwise not be discussed due to a stigma being attached to the disease; and encourages patient compliance with physician-directed treatment regimens.

Given the progress that continues to be made in society's battle against disease, patients are seeking more information about medical problems and potential treatments. The purpose of DTC advertising is to foster an informed conversation about health, disease and treatments between patients and their health care practitioners. Our Guiding Principles are an important step in ensuring patients and health care professionals get the information they need to make informed health care decisions.

CHAPTER 3

Do Prescription Drugs in America Cost Too Much?

The Rising Cost of Prescription Drugs: An Overview

Kaiser Family Foundation

The Kaiser Family Foundation is a nonprofit, privately operating organization that focuses on major health-care issues facing the United States.

Prescription drugs are vital to preventing and treating illness and helping to avoid more costly medical problems. Rising costs and implementation of the Medicare drug benefit have highlighted the need for a better understanding of the pharmaceutical market and for new approaches to address rising costs.

Rising Expenditures for Prescription Drugs

Spending in the US for prescription drugs was $200.7 billion in 2005, almost 5 times more than the $40.3 billion spent in 1990. Although prescription drug spending has been a relatively small proportion of national health care spending compared to spending for hospital and physician services (10% in 2005, compared to 31% and 21%, respectively), it has been one of the fastest growing components, increasing from 1994 to 2003 at double-digit rates compared to single-digit rates for hospital and physician services. However, the annual rate of increase in prescription spending declined from a high of 18% in 1999 to 6% in 2005, which is slightly lower than the 8% increase for hospital care and 7% for physician services in 2005. Prescription spending growth declined because of the slow-

Kaiser Family Foundation, "Prescription Drug Trends" fact sheet, www.kff.org, May, 2007. This information was reprinted with permission from the Henry J. Kaiser Family Foundation. The Kaiser Family Foundation, based in Menlo Park, California, is a non-profit, private operating foundation focusing on the major health care issues facing the nation and is not associated with Kaiser Permanente or Kaiser Industries.

down in Medicaid drug spending, the increased use of generic drugs (driven in part by the proliferation of tiered copayment benefit plans), changes in the types of drugs used, and a decrease in the number of new drugs introduced.

The share of prescription drug expenses paid by private health insurance increased substantially over the past decade (from 26% in 1990 to 47% in 2005), contributing to a decline in the share that people pay out-of-pocket (from 56% in 1990 to 25% in 2005). However, HHS [U.S. Dept. of Health and Human Services] projects that the shares will change significantly in 2006 when private health insurance will drop to 42%, out-of-pocket will decline to 19%, and public funds, because of Medicare's new Part D prescription drug program, will increase to 39%. . . .

Factors Driving Changes in Prescription Spending

Three main factors drive changes in prescription drug spending: changes in the number of prescriptions dispensed (utilization), price changes, and changes in the types of drugs used.

From 1995 to 2002, pharmaceutical manufacturers were the nation's most profitable industry.

Utilization. From 1994 to 2005, the number of prescriptions purchased increased 71% (from 2.1 billion to 3.6 billion), compared to a US population growth of 9%. The average number of retail prescriptions per capita increased from 7.9 in 1994 to 12.4 in 2006. The percent of the population with a prescription drug expense in 2004 was 59% (for those under age 65) and 92% (for those 65 and older); the proportions of these populations with a drug expense has changed little since 1996, when they were 62% and 88%, respectively.

Price. Retail prescription prices (which reflect both manufacturer price changes for existing drugs and changes in use to newer, higher-priced drugs) increased an average of 7.5% a year from 1994 to 2006 (from an average price of $28.67 to $68.26), almost triple the average annual inflation rate of 2.6%. The average brand name prescription price was over 3 times the average generic price in 2006 ($111.02 vs. 32.23). Of the 2006 average retail prescription price of $68.26, the manufacturer received 78% of the cost, the retailer received 19%, and the wholesaler received 3%.

Changes in Types of Drugs Used. Prescription drug spending is affected when new drugs enter the market and when existing medications lose patent protection. New drugs can increase overall drug spending if they are used in place of older, less expensive medications; if they supplement rather than replace existing drugs treatments; or if they treat a condition not previously treated with drug therapy. New drugs can reduce drug spending if they come into the market at a lower price than existing drug therapies; this can occur when a new drug enters a therapeutic category with one or two dominant brand competitors. New drug use is affected by the number of new drugs (new molecular entities) approved by the US Food and Drug Administration; approvals have fluctuated over the past decade, with 53 approvals in 1996, 27 in 2000, 36 in 2004, and 22 in 2006.

Drug spending is also typically reduced when brand drugs lose patent protection and face competition from new, lower cost generic substitutes. According to an FDA analysis, on average for drugs sold from 1999 through 2004, the percentage that the generic price was of the brand price decreased as the number of generic competitors increased: 94% with 1 generic competitor, 26% with 10 generic competitors, falling to 13% with 15 competitors.

Approximately three-quarters of FDA-approved drugs have generic counterparts. In 2006, 20% of prescription drug sales and 63% of prescriptions dispensed were generic medicines. Generic sales grew by 22% and generic prescriptions dispensed grew by 13% from 2005 to 2006.

Advertising. Both prescription use and shifts to higher-priced drugs can be influenced by advertising. After a decade of increases, the total amount manufacturers spent on advertising declined 3.5% from 2004 to 2005 (from $11.9 billion to $11.4 billion). The share directed toward consumers increased 5% in 2005 (from $4.0 to $4.2 billion), while the share directed toward physicians declined by 8% (from $7.8 to $7.2 billion). Spending for consumer advertising in 2005 was over 5 times the amount spent in 1996 ($0.8 billion), while 2005 physician advertising was 2 times the 1996 amount ($3.5 billion). The FDA and Congress are considering changes to prescription advertising rules.

Uninsured adults are twice as likely as insured adults to say that they or a family member cut pills, did not fill a prescription, or skipped medical treatment in the past year because of the cost.

Profitability. From 1995 to 2002, pharmaceutical manufacturers were the nation's most profitable industry. They ranked 3rd in 2003 and 2004, 5th in 2005, and in 2006 they ranked 2nd, with profits (return on revenues) of 19.6% compared to 6.3% for all Fortune 500 firms.

Insurance Coverage for Prescription Drugs

Lack of insurance coverage for prescription drugs can have adverse effects. A 2005 survey found that uninsured adults are twice as likely as insured adults to say that they or a family member cut pills, did not fill a prescription, or skipped medical treatment in the past year because of the cost (51% vs. 25%, respectively). Prescription drug coverage comes from a variety of private and public sources.

Employer Coverage. Employers are the principal source of health insurance in the United States, providing coverage for 177 million (60%) of Americans in 2005. Sixty-one percent of employers offered health insurance to their employees in 2006, and 65% of employees in those firms are covered by their employer's health plan. Other employees may have obtained coverage through a spouse. Nearly all (98%) of covered workers in employer-sponsored plans had a prescription drug benefit in 2006.

Medicare. Prior to January 1, 2006, the traditional Medicare program (the federal health program for the elderly and disabled) did not provide coverage for outpatient prescription drugs. As a result, about one-quarter (27%) of seniors age 65 and older, and one-third of poor (34%) and near-poor (33%) seniors, had no drug coverage in 2003. The Medicare Prescription Drug, Improvement, and Modernization Act of 2003 established a voluntary Medicare outpatient prescription drug benefit (known as Part D), effective January 1, 2006, under which the 44 million Medicare beneficiaries can enroll in private drug plans. These plans vary in benefit design, covered drugs, and utilization management strategies.

Department of Health and Human Services (HHS) data show that as of January 16, 2007, approximately 90% of all Medicare beneficiaries had drug coverage. . . .

Health plans have responded to increasing prescription drug costs by excluding certain drugs from coverage, using quantity dispensing limits, and increasing enrollee cost-sharing amounts.

Medicaid. Medicaid is the joint federal-state program that pays for medical assistance to over 55 million low-income individuals. Medicaid contributed 19% of total US drug spending in 2005 and is the major source of outpatient pharmacy services to the low-income population. All state Medicaid programs provide coverage for prescription drugs, although there are important differences in state policies with regard to co-payments, types of drugs that are covered, and the number of prescriptions that can be filled. The approximately 6 million dual eligibles who were transferred from Medicaid drug coverage to Medicare Part D drug coverage in January 2006 represented an estimated 14% of Medicaid beneficiaries and accounted for about 45% of Medicaid prescription drug spending in FY [fiscal year] 2003. Since January 1, 2006, states are required to make payments to Medicare to help finance Medicare drug coverage for the transferred and future dual eligibles.

Responses to Increasing Prescription Costs

Public and private health plans have implemented a variety of strategies to attempt to contain their rising costs for prescription drugs, as described below.

Utilization Management Strategies. Health plans have responded to increasing prescription drug costs by excluding certain drugs from coverage, using quantity dispensing limits, and increasing enrollee cost-sharing amounts. . . .

Discounts and Rebates. Private and public drug programs negotiate with pharmaceutical manufacturers (often using contracted organizations known as pharmacy benefit managers) to receive discounts and rebates which are applied based on volume, prompt payment, and market share. Manufacturers who want their drugs covered by Medicaid must provide rebates to state Medicaid programs for the drugs they purchase; many states have also negotiated additional rebates, known as supplemental rebates. However, the shift of the approximately 6 million dual eligibles from Medicaid to Medicare drug coverage affects the ability of state Medicaid programs to negotiate prices and secure supplemental rebates.

Several government agencies, including the Department of Veterans Affairs [VA], the Defense Department, the Public

Health Service, and the Coast Guard, participate in a program known as the Federal Supply Schedule through which they purchase drugs from manufacturers at prices equal to or lower than those charged to their "most-favored" nonfederal purchasers. In order to participate in Medicaid, the Section 304B Program requires manufacturers to provide drugs to certain nonfederal entities (such as community health centers and disproportionate share hospitals) at reduced prices.

Medicaid. Historically, prescription drugs have been one of the fastest-growing Medicaid services. Drug spending as a share of Medicaid spending on services rose from 5.6% in FY1992 to 13.4% in FY2003. A 2006 survey of 50 states+DC found that more than half had Medicaid pharmacy cost containment measures in place in FY2006, including preferred drug lists and prior authorization programs (about three-quarters of states), supplemental rebates from manufacturers (about 70% of states), and state Maximum Allowable Cost programs for generic and multi-source brand drugs (about 60%); smaller proportions of states were members of multi-state purchasing coalitions (about 25%) or had limits on quantities dispensed per prescription (about 20%).

Under the Deficit Reduction Act of 2005 (enacted 2/8/06), states were given more authority to control Medicaid drug spending through increased cost sharing for non-preferred drugs, changes in the way Medicaid pays pharmacists, allowing pharmacists to refuse prescriptions for beneficiaries who don't pay their cost sharing, and inclusion of authorized generic drugs in the calculation of "best price" for drugs.

Medicare. The Medicare Part D drug benefit shifts spending from the private sector and Medicaid to Medicare, making Medicare the nation's largest public payer of prescription drugs in 2006 when Medicare spending is projected to rise to 22% of total US prescription spending from 2% in 2005. . . .

In early 2007, the 110th Congress considered but did not pass legislation to allow or require Medicare to negotiate drug prices with drug makers.

Consumers are turning to a variety of methods to reduce their prescription costs, including requesting cheaper drugs or generic drugs from their physicians.

Purchasing Pools. Some private and public organizations have banded together to form prescription drug purchasing pools to increase their purchasing power through higher volume and shared expertise. Examples include the Department of Defense and VA joint purchasing from manufacturers; individual state purchasing pools for their Medicaid, state employees, senior/low-income/uninsured pharmacy assistance programs, or other public programs; and multi-state pools.

Consumer Tactics

Consumers. Consumers are turning to a variety of methods to reduce their prescription costs, including requesting cheaper drugs or generic drugs from their physicians, using the Internet and other sources to make price comparisons, buying over-the-counter instead of prescribed drugs, buying drugs in bulk and pill-splitting, using mail-order pharmacies, and using pharmaceutical company or state drug assistance programs. Over half of physicians say they frequently talk with patients about the out-of-pocket costs of medicines they prescribe, 62% say they switch patients to less expensive drugs, and 58% say they give patients office samples.

Importation. The high cost of prescriptions has led some to suggest that individuals be permitted to purchase prescription products from distributors in Canada or other countries (called "importation," or "reimportation"). Although it is generally not lawful for individuals or commercial entities such as pharmacies or wholesalers to purchase prescription drugs from other countries, the government does not always act to stop individuals from purchasing drug products abroad. Importation of pharmaceutical products from Canada through Internet sales and travel to Canada totaled about $700 million in sales in 2003, or 0.3% of total US prescription sales. An equivalent amount of prescription drugs was estimated to have entered the US from the rest of the world, mostly through the mail and courier services. Actual savings amounts, drug safety, and marketplace competition and pricing are issues being debated.

Many People Cannot Afford the Prices Set by the Profit-Driven Drug Industry

Katharine Greider

Katharine Greider is a journalist who focuses on health and medical topics. She is the author of The Big Fix: How the Pharmaceutical Industry Rips Off Consumers.

Researchers studying the moral development of children sometimes ask them to consider a hypothetical proposition known as the Heinz dilemma. It goes like this: Heinz's wife is very sick. If she doesn't get a certain medicine, she's sure to die. The trouble is, the medicine's so costly Heinz can't possibly afford it. Should he steal the medicine to save his wife?

In recent years especially, this dilemma has escaped the confines of the psych lab and has landed in the living rooms of countless ordinary Americans. As month after month seniors and younger working people across the country anxiously go over their budgets and wonder how they'll beg, borrow, or steal enough to pay for their medicines, they're undergoing a moral education of their own. Ever more insistently, they're asking new questions: What gives these drug companies the right to charge so much? And just what are we getting for our money?

Drug companies make something we want and need: medicines that promise to protect us from pain and illness, that safeguard our ability to keep our routines at work and at home. The pharmaceutical industry can claim for its products seemingly magical benefits, from making us look better to literally saving our lives. Behind these magical claims lies a complex product whose merits are not easily evaluated by scientists, much less consumers. Even the most alert consumers are not equipped with the necessary information or power to decide what medicine they'll take and at what price, but must rely on layers of expert middlemen—from the U.S. Food and Drug Administration (FDA), which approves drugs for marketing; to the insurance organizations that pay for medicines; to the physician who alone has the power to order a drug. All this puts the drug industry in a unique position to exploit its customers with high prices and seductive marketing. And that, in the absence of government actions to curtail their activities, is just what they're doing.

Some pharmaceutical giants have resorted to unethical (or outright illegal) tactics to extend patents on their top sellers.

Struggling to Pay for Medicine

Meet the McCuddys of Ohio. Five years ago [in 1998] Melva McCuddy, seventy-seven, didn't need much medicine: an aspirin before bed to protect her heart. Then in late 1999, she learned she had breast cancer, and her health problems—and drug bills—mushroomed. She was diagnosed with type 2 diabetes. She had two angioplasties and, ultimately, a mastectomy. Not only was she reeling from the trauma of losing her health, but suddenly she had to come up with more than $500 a month to buy medicines, including tamoxifen to prevent recurrence of the breast cancer, the diabetes drug Glucophage XR, the calcium channel-blocker Norvasc for blood pressure, and an antidepressant to help her cope with "this whole mess," which was soon compounded by the death of her mother.

Melva manages. Although she has no insurance coverage for prescriptions, a modest pension from her late husband

William's job as a newspaper photographer supplements social security, and she takes a bus to Canada, where prescription drugs are much cheaper. But she is upset. She worked, supervising university field research, into her seventies—even took freelance jobs while she was home raising three kids—and William worked steadily from the time he returned from his post as an aerial photographer in World War II. "It just kills me," she says. "For those of us who went through the depression, through the wars . . . well it goes through your mind that you have worked all your life for the profits of the pharmaceutical companies."

Drugmakers have become deeply enmeshed in the process that determines which drugs Americans use, and when, and why, and how we use them.

Get Melva on the subject of prescription drug costs, and before long she's liable to mention her son: She worries about him. A self-employed realtor, Jim McCuddy, fifty, had a severe heart attack two years ago and endures a host of related chronic conditions, including worsening asthma and depression, that have him on a dozen prescription medications; some are pricey new bestsellers. Jim recently discovered his insurance premiums were going up to almost $700 a month; he just doesn't have the money, so he has dropped his prescription coverage. And what about the $900 monthly cost of his medicines? "I can't pay it," he says gloomily. "Luckily my doctor has been helping me out with some samples, but if those run out I don't know what I'm going to do. I guess I'll have to talk to him about getting rid of some of my prescriptions. Hopefully it won't kill me."

And like his mom, Jim worries about his own son, twenty-eight-year-old James W. McCuddy; last winter he started vomiting blood—an ulcer. His two brand-name prescription drugs cost about $200 a month. That may not seem like a lot. But

Jimmy works as a cook for $8 an hour, with no benefits. "It takes a week's check to buy his prescriptions," says his father.

The McCuddys' struggle to pay for medicine—and that of the millions who share their predicament—could hardly fail to win our sympathy. But making drugs is expensive, right? Well, yes and no. A recent study of six representative drug-makers' financial reports found they spent only 43 percent of revenues to research, develop, and manufacture their products. A very hefty slice of the McCuddys' pharmaceutical dollar comes right back at them in the form of promotional campaigns that relentlessly push the newest, hottest, and most expensive drugs, be they lifesavers or duds. Meanwhile, some pharmaceutical giants have resorted to unethical (or outright illegal) tactics to extend patents on their top sellers, cutting off competition from low-cost generics the McCuddys might be better able to afford. And while the industry's trade group casts it as a patient advocate working to eradicate disease and defend the public's right to "access" drugs, the ferocity of its lobbyists is largely dedicated to defending drugmakers' right to charge whatever they please in the most lucrative drug market in the world. Melva is right on the money when she talks about profits: The drug industry is the most profitable of any in America and has been at or near the top for a generation.

Drug Company Tactics

But this is about more than just prices and profits. In pursuit of the latter—a natural and potentially productive pursuit for any industry—drugmakers have become deeply enmeshed in the process that determines which drugs Americans use, and when, and why, and how we use them. As the principal funders of drug research, pharmaceutical companies today enjoy an unprecedented level of control over what we learn about their products; they formulate the research questions according to their needs, and they supply the answers. Visiting drug salesmen are often a doctor's main source of information about new medicines. Drug companies also sponsor (and sometimes design) many of the classes physicians take to continue their licenses. In some specialties, nearly every influential expert has financial ties to the drugmakers that dominate their field. Over the last five years, the industry has also demonstrated its mastery in consumer advertising, enlisting in its sales push our own vanities, hopes, fears, and doubts. In the process of broadening their markets, drug companies sponsor "disease awareness" campaigns through patient advocacy groups and celebrity spokespeople, influencing how we define illness and where we look for relief. Through so-called user fees, the drug industry even pays the salaries of FDA staff who approve or reject their applications for new drugs.

To create the outsized sales figures characteristic of a blockbuster, a drug typically has to be sold at a high price, for "chronic" or long-term use, to a vast number of people.

Whatever a drug company does—whether a drug trial lasting years or a thirty-second TV spot—it does to make money. Why else? In this respect it is no different from the sellers of soda pop or soap flakes. But drugs aren't soap flakes; here, it's not just our economic interests at stake but the integrity of our health system, and, ultimately, our health itself. To justify its practices in everything from pricing to marketing, the industry's spokespeople put across the self-serving notion that what's good for the drug business is good for the public health—is good for the McCuddys. They would have us believe that the industry research is designed not primarily to develop lucrative products and position them advantageously in the marketplace, but to save lives. Its exhaustive sales pitch is really "education." With drugs becoming a more expensive and, indeed, a more important tool in preventing and treating disease, can we afford to let these assertions go unchallenged?

A Critical Problem

It may be that given our faith in the twin forces of technology and an unfettered marketplace, Americans are particularly susceptible to the drug industry's reasoning. Whatever the case, the industry's excesses are an American problem that is reaching critical proportions. Among the wealthy nations that support the global pharmaceutical industry, the United States is by far the most permissive in its regulatory scheme. As other countries move to control prices and sharply limit advertising, the industry increasingly turns to American consumers for its profits. Meanwhile, America is facing a harsh economic downturn that makes it less fit to bear this burden. State and federal budgets are no longer so ample, making for bitter debates about how to control drug costs in government programs like Medicaid and Medicare. People are losing their jobs and insurance benefits. Like Jim McCuddy, they're suddenly feeling the pain of two decades of price escalation.

What they may not understand is that they're also suffering the consequences of a voracious and unsustainable business model. Over the last couple of decades, the pharmaceutical industry has consolidated dramatically and has garnered a larger and larger share of its profits from a relatively small number of new, high-margin "blockbuster" products. To create the outsized sales figures characteristic of a blockbuster, a drug typically has to be sold at a high price, for "chronic" or long-term use, to a vast number of people. This can rarely be achieved without very intensive promotional efforts. But blockbusters are not immortal; indeed, the bigger the blockbuster, the more revenue disappears when the drug loses patent protection or sustains some other killing blow—say, a serious and unexpected side effect emerges. Meanwhile, the larger the company, the more excess sales dollars it has to produce each year to meet investors' demand for steep and steady earnings growth. Just to keep up, the big players must generate a steady stream of new blockbusters—new drugs that can be sold at high enough prices and to large enough swaths of population to bring in billions in annual sales. The trouble is, this is a requirement of the drug industry, not of public health. Company X's new allergy medicine may not justify that American consumers be parted from billions of their hard-earned dollars—a situation that in many cases only stimulates a redoubling of Company X's marketing efforts. And so the cycle, which lately has taken on a frenzied air, begins anew. . . .

We might think of the drug industry's territory as a broad swatch of land covered by dense thickets. Here is the science of pharmacology; over there, the arcana of patent law. On one hand are the complex workings of the federal government; on the other, the quicksilver messages of Madison Avenue. The field of medical research is the purview of one group of experts, quite separate from the economics of pricing. The drug industry relies on the expectation that few nonexperts who venture into these intricacies will find their footing. But ordinary Americans can navigate this landscape and emerge with confidence. Although some of the facts may seem obscure, the big picture—the utter folly of allowing a profit-driven industry to name its price, while quietly making over our public-health agenda in its own image—is hidden in broad daylight.

Importing Less-Costly Prescription Drugs from Abroad Should Be Allowed

Nelda Barnett

Nelda Barnett is a member of AARP's national board of directors.

Prescription drug costs continue to rise. Recent reports estimate that total spending on health care is expected to double by 2016, and much of this is due to rising prescription drug costs.

A recent AARP [an organization of people over 50 years of age] study revealed that, on average, pharmaceutical manufacturer prices for the 193 brand name drugs most widely used by older Americans rose at nearly twice the rate of general inflation in 2006. Reversing the trend between 2004 and 2005, when the average rate of increase in manufacturer drug prices fell, the 2006 average growth rate of 6.2 percent represents an up-tick from the 2005 average increase of 6.0 percent. For the 153 brand-name drugs that were on the market since 2000, this translates into a cumulative average price increase of 53.6 percent, over two-and-one-half times the general inflation rate of 20.1 percent over the same period.

The new Medicare prescription drug benefit is helping tens of millions of Medicare beneficiaries better afford their prescription drugs. However, even with this new program, Medicare beneficiaries are still feeling the effects of rising prescription drug costs in the form of the higher premiums, deductibles, co-payments and—for some beneficiaries—lack of coverage in the donut hole.

Medicare beneficiaries are not the only group impacted by rising prescription drug prices. Escalating prescription drug

Nelda Barnett, testimony before the U.S. Senate Committee on Commerce, Science, and Transportation, http://commerce.senate.gov, March 7, 2007.

prices continue to hamper employers' ability to provide health insurance coverage for their workers and families. In addition employers are increasingly eliminating or curtailing their retiree prescription drug coverage.

Pressures also continue to squeeze public programs at both the state and federal level. Rising drug prices also plague Medicaid, and put pressure on states' ability to maintain current coverage levels. These prices also hamper states' ability to expand eligibility to meet the increasing need as fewer employers provide access to affordable health care coverage.

It is a national embarrassment that people from all over the world come to the United States to access our advanced medical systems while many of our own citizens need to look outside our borders in order to afford their prescription drugs.

Finally, rising prescription drug prices particularly hurt the almost 47 million Americans who lack health insurance. These individuals pay among the highest prices in the world for their prescription drug needs. Some don't fill prescriptions because they cannot afford to do so.

Public Support for Importation Grows

For the millions of Americans without drug coverage and those with limited coverage, importation is seen as an option to obtain access to affordable medications. A recent AARP poll found that AARP members overwhelmingly support Congress allowing for the importation of drugs from Canada and Europe. While AARP does not believe prescription drug importation is the sole solution to soaring drug prices in the United States, we do believe it is one way to begin to secure lower priced drugs.

Our members and their families question why brand name drug prices in Canada and other industrialized countries can be lower—sometimes by as much as 50 percent lower—than prices in the United States. It is a national embarrassment that people from all over the world come to the United States to access our advanced medical systems while many of our own citizens need to look outside our borders in order to afford their prescription drugs.

The simple fact is that importation is already happening. In 2003, Americans purchased approximately 12 million prescription drug products (valued at almost $700 million) from Canada alone. As prescription drug prices continue to rise, more and more individuals are choosing to import prescription drugs. We have a responsibility to ensure that Americans who choose to import prescription drugs do so safely. Congress can no longer afford to do nothing but hope that the millions of Americans who purchase prescription drugs from abroad do so without dire consequences.

We believe that Congress should enact legislation that provides appropriate safeguards while at the same time ensuring a workable system for prescription drug importation. Currently, many prescription drugs sold for market in the U.S. are already manufactured abroad and brought into the U.S. safely and legally by prescription drug manufacturers. If these manufacturers can import drugs safely and legally, then a process can be created to allow American consumers to safely import drugs.

New Cancer Drugs Cost More than Their Brief Extending of Life May Be Worth

Daniel Costello

Daniel Costello is a staff writer for the Los Angeles Times.

What is the value of a few months of life?

That question is at the center of one of the most controversial debates in medicine today involving a new generation of hyper-expensive cancer drugs.

[In March 2007] the Food and Drug Administration approved GlaxoSmithKline's Tykerb, a once-a-day pill for late-stage breast cancer patients that costs nearly $35,000 a year. It's the latest of half a dozen new cancer therapies with names such as Avastin and Tarceva that can run as much as $100,000 for an annual supply.

Although the medications work much longer in some patients, they help extend the lives of most for only a few months.

The drugs' sky-high costs compared with their relatively small health benefits have sparked arguments among policy-makers and medical professionals about what to do with the growing number of people who are depleting their life savings on the drugs or, worse, who can't get them at all. More broadly, they ask, is this the best way for society to spend its increasingly limited healthcare dollars?

Harriet and Mort Frank illustrate the ethical and financial dilemmas. Since December [2006], the retired Mission Viejo [CA] couple have been paying as much as $2,000 a month in out-of-pocket costs for Harriet's lymphoma medication, Rituxan, by Genentech Inc. and Biogen Idec Inc. The Franks get by on $1,432 a month with their combined Social Security checks and a small amount of savings. But with the drug's expense eating into their modest nest egg, they're worried about what might happen next.

Traditionally, drug companies have said the prices of their drugs are based on the costs to develop them. Now, they say, drugs are priced according to what the market will bear.

"So far this medication is working wonders," Mort said. "But I keep thinking, how are we going to keep affording it?"

High Cost for Small Benefits

Drug companies and many patients insist even incremental gains are worthwhile. Small clinical advances are likely to turn into larger ones over time, and patients who can afford the treatments say they deserve them.

Traditionally, drug companies have said the prices of their drugs are based on the costs to develop them. Now, they say, drugs are priced according to what the market will bear. "The cost of our product incorporates both the extensive costs incurred during research and development as well as the price determined by the market," said Walter Moore, vice president of government affairs for Genentech in South San Francisco.

But doctors, patient advocates and healthcare economists warn that the drugs are simply too expensive at a time when medical costs are rising rapidly—and more patients are picking up a growing share of their medical bills.

The costs aren't borne only by those who are sick. Because insurers pay for almost all federally approved drugs, the costs of covering them would eventually spill into the nation's over-all medical bill and therefore would raise everyone's insurance premiums.

[In 2007], cancer drugs are expected to account for nearly 22% of the nation's drug bill, up from 13% in 2002, according to [investment firm] Morgan Stanley.

Oncologists . . . admit being torn about wanting to give patients marginally effective drugs that could cause serious financial harm.

Several countries, including Britain, refuse to pay for the drugs for all patients. Here, Congress is considering legislation to control the costs of biotech drugs.

The debate also is raging among oncologists [cancer doctors], who admit being torn about wanting to give patients marginally effective drugs that could cause serious financial harm. "These drugs are good, but it's important to remember they aren't a cure," said Peter Eisenberg, an oncologist at California Cancer Center in Greenbrae, Calif. "Drug companies are in another world if they think people can afford these things."

Dr. Edith Perez, co-director of the breast cancer center at the Mayo Clinic, said some patients with insurance were paying thousands of dollars for the therapies.

Doctors Are Concerned

Because many patients now pay as much as 30% of their medical bills rather than flat co-payments, some physicians have started offering payment plans for patients who rack up bills as high as tens of thousands of dollars, Perez said.

In the current issue of the *Journal of the American Medical Assn.*, a general practitioner from Oklahoma City described his experience with the lack of uniform access to new cancer drugs. In a one-page commentary, Dr. Perry Klaassen, 66, wrote how he was diagnosed with colon cancer in 2001 and was surviving because of a series of cancer drugs he has taken regularly since then. He pays $450 a month, which he described in an interview as manageable.

One of his patients wasn't so lucky. [In 2004], Klaassen diagnosed a 63-year-old woman with late-stage colon cancer. He recommended that she try chemotherapy and other drugs, but she declined, saying she didn't have insurance and didn't want to burden her family with unneeded debt. She died a year later.

"We have to be able to do better than this," Klaassen said. . . .

Prices Are Steep

As recently as a decade ago, cancer therapies rarely cost more than a $1,000 a year. But they weren't very effective and had harmful side effects. The newer, so-called targeted drugs work like Trojan horses, slipping inside cancer cells and attacking them without killing lots of healthy cells. Although some patients on the new cancer drugs such as Gleevec, a leukemia drug made by Novartis Inc., live significantly longer, most lives are extended for just a few months.

Nonetheless, the prices are steep. When Herceptin, the first targeted therapy that treats breast cancer, arrived in 1998, it cost about $20,000 for a typical cycle.

All of the drugs' price tags jumped considerably by 2004, when ImClone Inc. and Bristol-Myers Squibb Co. introduced Erbitux, a late-stage colorectal-cancer therapy that costs about $10,000 a month. Drug companies point out that some late-stage cancer patients don't survive on therapy for long and use less than a year of treatment.

Tykerb, GlaxoSmithKline's breast cancer drug, costs slightly less than most targeted drugs, but it extends the lives of most patients only about two months. A trial of 399 women given Tykerb along with chemotherapy showed that it stopped the progression of tumors in patients for nearly seven months versus about five months for those on chemotherapy alone. Soon, such drugs may grow in popularity. Although most are now used solely in late-stage cancer patients, some are being approved to treat early-stage cancer, potentially expanding their use significantly.

[In 2006], the Food and Drug Administration approved Herceptin for women who were in remission and Genentech's Avastin for earlier-stage colorectal cancer. Many drug companies also are trying to expand the use of targeted drugs.

That could quickly turn several of the drugs into some of the top-selling medications in the world, raising healthcare costs overall.

Analysts expect Avastin's sales to reach $7 billion in the U.S. by 2009, compared with $1.1 billion in 2005.

Reshaping Cancer Treatment

The targeted cancer drugs and better detection are helping reshape cancer treatment, leading some to believe a corner has been turned in the fight against the disease. [In 2006], cancer deaths fell for a second straight year. Three out of five cancer patients now live at least five years after their diagnosis, and there are now 10 million cancer survivors in the U.S., according to the National Cancer Society.

Some of the new cancer drugs may not be worth their costs when measured against their benefit.

But those gains have to be taken in context of what else the money spent on cancer treatment could have been used for, said Peter Neumann, director of the Center for the Evaluation of Value and Risk at Tufts-New England Medical Center. "In terms of the cost of a life saved, it's possible other areas of medicine, like better disease prevention or better cardiovascular care, may be more effective."

Although it's a vague metric, one historical tool used to judge the value of a medical intervention is known as the Quality Adjusted Life Year, which is essentially a rule of thumb that a year of prolonged life is worth around $50,000 in today's dollars. By that standard, some of the new cancer drugs may not be worth their costs when measured against their benefit to society, Neumann said.

Increasingly, advocate groups such as Breast Cancer Action in San Francisco are pushing Congress to pass laws limiting the price drug makers can charge for such drugs. The recent pressure, however, appears to be having an effect on the companies themselves. [In 2006], when Amgen Inc. won approval for a new colon cancer drug, Vectibix, which costs $8,000 a month, the Thousand Oaks [CA]–based company said patients would receive it free after co-payments exceeded 5% of their adjusted gross income.

Soon after, Genentech unveiled its own plan. The biotech company said it would impose a cap of $55,000 per patient per year no matter their income or insurance status.

High Prices of Drugs
for Minor Problems
Pay for Drugs That Cure
More Serious Ones

Peter W. Huber

Peter W. Huber is a senior fellow at the Manhattan Institute for Policy Research and the author of many books.

The more our health depends on their little pills, the more we seem to hate big drug companies. In *The Constant Gardener* (2000), John le Carré assigns to the pharmaceutical industry the role played by the KGB in his earlier novels. A villainous pharmaceutical company is using Kenya as a testing ground for a lethally defective drug, and people who find out about it die, too. Four recent, non-fiction indictments of the industry tell a similar story. Conflating the four into one, one might title them collectively *How Big Pharma Deceives, Endangers, and Rips Us Off, with the Complicity of Doctors.*

Two of these books are by former editors of the prestigious *New England Journal of Medicine.* Slamming the drug companies, Marcia Angell argues that Big Pharma, as it has come to be called, "uses its wealth and power to co-opt every institution that might stand in its way, including the U.S. Congress, the Food and Drug Administration, academic medical centers, and the medical profession itself." Slamming the medical profession, academics, and professional organizations, Jerome P. Kassirer, Angell's former boss, labels them Big Pharma's "whores."

The bill of particulars, drawn from the books cited above, goes something like this. Most of what people believe about

Big Pharma is just "mythology spun by the industry's immense public-relations apparatus." Forget miracle drugs—Big Pharma is not a "research-based industry," it is "an idea-licensing, pharmaceutical-formulating-and-manufacturing, clinical-testing, patenting, and marketing industry." As for "the few innovative drugs that do come to market," these "nearly always stem from publicly supported research" or are developed by small biotech firms. Big Pharma simply goes "trolling small companies all over the world for drugs to license." At most, tweaking the chemistry of drugs developed by others, it advances medicine by "waiting for Godot."

Moreover, these me-too drugs "usually target very common lifelong conditions—like arthritis or depression or high blood pressure or elevated cholesterol." Many just aren't needed, because older drugs already work as well or better, or because the new drugs are peddled to people who aren't sick. Big Pharma is thus "primarily a marketing machine to sell drugs of dubious benefit."

Getting drug policy right depends mainly on getting [the] difference straight . . . between ministering to the sick and making medicines.

All the while, the industry neglects many essential drugs that treat uncommon diseases, transient conditions, or lethal conditions, or that provide immunity or quick, complete cures. Thus, in 2001 alone, there were "serious shortages" of certain anesthetics, anti-venoms, steroids for premature infants, antidotes for certain drug overdoses, an anti-clotting drug for hemophilia, an injectable drug used in cardiac resuscitation, an antibiotic for gonorrhea, a drug to induce labor in childbirth, and, worst of all, childhood vaccines. In general, the industry is "supremely uninterested" in tropical diseases and other afflictions of the very poor. We get Viagra. They get malaria.

Then there is the pricing—always the pricing. . . .

A Steep Slope

So runs the indictment. Now for a story. In an April 2005 obituary, the *New York Times* described Maurice Hilleman as the man who "probably saved more lives than any other scientist in the 20th century." What kind of genius does it take to get that on your tombstone? Hilleman himself, it seems, "credited much of his success to his boyhood work with chickens." He went on to use fertilized chicken eggs to grow large quantities of bacteria and viruses that were then weakened or killed to produce vaccines. . . .

Whether the first pill typically costs $100 million or $1 billion to develop, replicating it costs less—a thousand times less, or perhaps a million times less.

By farming eggs, Maurice Hilleman saved tens of millions of lives, and prevented deafness, blindness, and other permanent disabilities among many millions more. No [humanitarian doctor] Albert Schweitzer or [famed nurse] Florence Nightingale could ever post numbers like his. Doctors and nurses save lives one on one, and are paid by the hour. Hilleman saved lives by the carton, at grocery-store prices—acres of cartons, hundreds of millions of warm eggs replicating his genius around the clock.

Getting drug policy right depends mainly on getting that difference straight—the difference, that is, between ministering to the sick and making medicines—and grasping its implications from the start. Big Pharma's critics do not even try.

Pricing is indeed the key. Whether the first pill typically costs $100 million or $1 billion to develop, replicating it costs less—a thousand times less, or perhaps a million times less. This slope—precipice, really—is far steeper than most of the other hills and valleys of economic life. It complicates things immeasurably. It also largely explains the gulf between the industry's perception of reality and that of the critics. . . .

The cliff is still higher if you compare the cost of manufacturing the last pill that rolls out of the factory against its value to the person who desperately needs it. A generation or two ago, the diseases that would be rubbed out by Hilleman's green thumb cost humanity countless billions in lost productivity, premature death, and time spent attending to the sick. Hilleman's egg farms saved lives at pennies a shot. . . .

Big Pharma's critics have much to say about Merck's Vioxx . . . that, because of suspected side effects, was pulled from the market in 2004. They rarely mention the company's vaccines.

Viewed from the pill-in-hand perspective, the precipice supports what the critics demand—vaccines for pennies, not billions, prices pegged to the cost of the last pill, not the first. And that is indeed the economically efficient and socially desirable price to set—*after* a Hilleman has worked his magic, after you have the first egg, the first pill, securely in hand. But if you peg all prices to last-pill costs, you will not get another $2 trillion or so of private capital searching for another Hilleman—who, by the way, worked his magic at [pharmaceutical giant] Merck. Big Pharma's critics have much to say about Merck's Vioxx, the arthritis painkiller that, because of suspected side effects, was pulled from the market in 2004. They rarely mention the company's vaccines.

How a Beauty Cream Saves Lives

The best solution, if you can pull it off, is to charge both more and less at the same time. Sometimes you can.

A drug called eflornithine was developed in the 1970's to treat cancer. It didn't suppress cancer very well—but it did, unexpectedly, cure something else: sleeping sickness. Endemic in many parts of Africa, sleeping sickness (trypanosomiasis) is the second most deadly parasitic disease on the planet.

(Malaria is first.) Treated with eflornithine, the near-dead sleepers arise, take up their pallets, and walk.

But they are too poor to pay on the way out. In 1999, the manufacturer stopped producing the drug. It licensed the formula to the World Health Organization (WHO), but no other company was willing to make it. The reason was obvious: sub-Saharan Africa cannot cover even the second-pill cost of manufacturing Western drugs to Western standards. And the really poor, or those that assist them, can barely afford the last-pill cost.

Then Bristol-Myers-Squibb discovered that eflornithine impedes the growth of women's facial hair, and began marketing it in a beauty cream called Vaniqa. The company that still controlled the rights gave the WHO $25 million—enough for a five-year supply, at last-pill prices, plus research, surveillance, and training of health-care workers. Yes, the rich get Viagra, and Vaniqa too. The poor still get malaria, but they can now beat trypanosomiasis. . . .

The Value of "Unnecessary" Drugs

As for Big Pharma's addiction to *un*necessary medications, Angell would have the FDA review not only the safety and efficacy of each new drug but also the public's need for it. She questions whether many drugs are needed at all. The companies, she contends, "promote diseases to fit their drugs," redefining the "high" in "cholesterol" or "blood pressure," the "dysfunction" in "erectile," the "dysphoric" in menses, and the "normal" in "aging." She also believes that new drugs are often worse than the old ones they replace. The FDA, she argues, should license a drug only upon a showing that it is materially better than what is already available.

In practice, this would create an enormous bias in favor of the first drug through the gate. Establishing efficacy is a very large undertaking, even in tests against a placebo. For later arrivals, the far higher cost of testing drug against drug would crush incremental improvements completely. It would also cut off the possibility of discovering that a second-best pill for a first disease is the first-best pill for a second. Eflornithine performed worse than other cancer drugs, and unwanted facial hair is a normal incident of female aging. No drug company ever would have bothered to submit *this* drug to Angell's FDA.

Big drug companies shun some drugs and embrace others because, collectively, the FDA, doctors, patients, insurers, and juries push costs higher, and prices lower, on some categories of drugs and not on others.

Much of the conduct described by Angell and other critics rings true, because it sounds like a rational response to economic reality. It is the critics' explanation of motives that fails to persuade. Why do big drug companies compete fiercely to supply what we don't much need, but not what we really need? Because, comes the response, they are greedy and profitable, spending huge amounts to flack their unneeded products, and jacking up their prices to cover all those unnecessary costs.

Industry flacks do indeed spend a great deal to sell us better sex and thinner thighs. But does that mean they also contrive to suppress demand drugs to induce labor, steroids for premature infants, or childhood vaccines? The more plausible story is that big drug companies shun some drugs and embrace others because, collectively, the FDA, doctors, patients, insurers, and juries push costs higher, and prices lower, on some categories of drugs and not on others, to the point where some make economic sense and some do not. Universities and small biotechs license their innovations to Big Pharma because they lack the capital, scale, and expertise required for mass manufacturing, because they wouldn't know how to sell the same drug five times in succession (to the FDA, doctors, patients, insurers, and juries), and because a vast and swampy system separates pharmaceutical innovation from the treatment of real patients at prices that will cover cost and earn a profit. The little guys just don't have what it takes to finish the job. . . .

Few companies manufacture vaccines, because vaccines are so essential that they are sold mainly to the government, at reasonable-and-uniform—which is to say rock-bottom—prices, and because the seller may well be bankrupted by lawsuits if a problem is uncovered only after tens of millions of healthy people have been vaccinated.

Pharma's biochemical cures always end up far cheaper than the people-centered services they ultimately displace.

The critics say that pricing complexity is so much fog, created by big drug companies in order to hide what they spend seducing regulators and academics, corrupting doctors, and beguiling patients. The industry's economic fundamentals suggest precisely the opposite. Fog is essential to sustain price discrimination—which is good, not bad, when the first pill costs a million times more than the last. Many small drug companies, government labs, and academics pursue drugs we really need. Aid organizations like WHO were keenly interested in getting eflornithine to Africa. But none could get it there, not for love or money. That required Vaniqa.

Drugs Cost Less than Services

Today's health-care dollars mainly buy not drugs but time and beds. Hospital care accounts for about 30 percent of on-budget health spending; physician and clinical services account for another 20 percent. The money pays mainly for manual labor—the cost of one person laying hands on another, working from the outside in, with the medical equivalents of wheelbarrows, shovels, and picks. There are no cost cliffs in this line of work. When the matron pays her plastic surgeon in New York, he doesn't throw in a free resurrection for the afflicted in [the African city of] Ouagadougou.

Prescription drugs currently account for well under 20 percent of the health-care budget. Within a generation or two, they will undoubtedly account for most of it—which will be another good thing. Pharma's biochemical cures always end up far cheaper than the people-centered services they ultimately displace. Moreover, while much hands-on care only drags things out or soothes, the best medicines really cure. It is true that, early on in the pharmacological assault on a grave disease, drugs also stretch things out and can fail to beat the disease, so we often end up buying more drug and more doctor, too. But eventually drugs improve to the point where they beat the disease and thus lay off both doctor and hospital. . . .

Big Government makes health care fair, transparent, and reasonable by making it flat. Big Pharma exploits the cliffs and valleys of Vaniqa economics. Big Government makes collective calls about safety, efficacy, cost, and insurance coverage. Big Pharma tweaks, tinkers, packages, and brands in order to load the pharmacy's shelves with mind-numbing arrays of very similar medicines sold at very different prices. Flat drug prices are not good for us; price spreads, wide enough to cover first-pill costs and meet last-pill pocketbooks, are good for us.

Biochemical tweaking is good for us, too. People and their diseases vary, often in small ways. Biochemical effects are hard to predict. Even trivial changes can make big differences, and medical progress often depends on trial and error. Developed for insomniacs, thalidomide now treats leprosy. First revealed in the human womb, the drug's extraordinary power to halt cell division also holds promise in the treatment of brain and breast cancer, macular degeneration in the eye, and immune-system diseases. AIDS patients organized buyers' clubs to bootleg the drug from Brazil because of its powerful effect on the immune system. Drugs and drug cocktails are now being matched to genotype. Stem-cell scientists are moving beyond chickens and mice to cultivate genetically customized therapies from human ovaries.

Over the last decade, extraordinary advances in bioengineering have transformed pharmacology. Sooner or later, the industry and its pilot fish will surely find drugs that can halt colon, breast, and lung cancers, that can curb obesity and thus heart disease, and that will not merely suppress the H1V virus but purge it from the body completely. A new pharmacology of the brain may cure depression and stop the onset of Alzheimer's. These and other once inscrutable scourges are now—essentially—becoming problems in diligent engineering.

They are very difficult and expensive problems, as engineering problems go. And government funding did indeed pay for much of the underlying science, and continues to pay for it, just as the industry's critics charge. Some 600 publicly traded pharmaceutical and biotechnology companies worldwide, however, are now capitalized at over $1.5 trillion. The industry's critics would subordinate current management to public-utility regulation. We will fare better, much better, if we streamline regulation, curb litigation, and unleash prices to make vaccines as alluring to Big Pharma as Viagra and Vaniqa.

Medical Innovation Would Stop If the Government Controlled Drug Prices

Sidney Taurel

Sidney Taurel is the chairman and chief executive officer of Eli Lilly, a leading pharmaceutical company.

Let me start with a question: Do you believe we already have all the medical innovation we need?

That may sound like a purely rhetorical question, but it's not. For one thing, there are some influential commentators who are on record saying, in essence, "yes." Moreover, if actions can be taken as answers, I have to assume that many policymakers, here and in other nations, must agree with that view.

The two most important preconditions for innovation in my industry are market-based pricing and intellectual property protection. But when I look at health care systems around the world, I see that policies that support innovation are dwindling, while policies that discourage it are proliferating. A third-party observer trying to make sense of this, without access to other data on the motives involved, might reasonably conclude that this amounts to a worldwide campaign against pharmaceutical innovation.

These measures are almost always advocated and adopted in the name of cost control. I don't really believe that there is some global conspiracy or even that the proponents of any single measure actually intend to stop medical progress. Nonetheless, that may turn out to be their end effect. I have a real concern that, if these trends continue, especially here in the United States, we could see the collapse of true innovation in biomedicine. . . .

Sidney Taurel, "The Campaign Against Innovation," (speech), www.lilly.com, March 18, 2003. Reproduced by permission.

Incentives for Innovation Are Threatened

When all is said and done, there is only one market in the world that supports pharmaceutical innovation—the United States. We still speak of it as the "last free market," and indeed, though hardly "free" of government intervention, it is the one market where global innovators find the incentive they need to keep pushing the boundaries.

Under a regime of weaker [intellectual property] protection or harsher market controls, [the pharmaceutical industry's research & development] would no longer be able to deliver true innovation.

But those incentives are now threatened on a number of fronts, as various kinds of cost-control legislation find new proponents—notwithstanding Dr. [Frank] Lichtenberg's work showing that the benefits of new drugs greatly exceed their costs.

Congress has actually passed legislation to allow U.S. pharmacies to import U.S.-made drugs from Canadian wholesalers, essentially importing Canada's price controls as well. The only thing holding it back from implementation is FDA [U.S. Food and Drug Administration] concerns about potential safety problems.

We see many states adopting a variety of price measures and access controls to reduce their Medicaid drug costs. In some cases, they are trying to extend Medicaid drug rebates to a larger segment of their population. The debate over Medicare reform and especially over the addition of an outpatient drug benefit is in many ways a debate over a market-based model versus the current central planning approach, with its attendant price controls.

Finally, we've seen a variety of measures that would weaken intellectual property laws in the U.S. A bill was passed in the

Senate [in 2002] that would tilt the playing field heavily in favor of generic companies and very much against the research-oriented innovators.

Given the discouraging climate for innovation already established around the world, I believe that any of these more drastic proposals would, if implemented in the U.S., lead to a "death spiral" in our ability to find and develop new treatments.

When I make this point to elected officials, I realize that many don't believe me. Perhaps they hear it as a threat and think it's really a bluff. Perhaps they think it's just a gross exaggeration. Perhaps what they won't quite say out loud is roughly this: "Are you saying you'll stop doing R&D [research and development]? You won't. That's what you do. You don't have any other business to be in."

No company has ever found a way to produce big, innovative drugs efficiently, economically, or even predictably.

While it's true we would not turn out the lights in our labs—we would continue to do some form of R&D—but it would be very different than what we are doing today. My key point is that, under a regime of weaker IP [intellectual property] protection or harsher market controls, our R&D would no longer be able to deliver true innovation.

Blockbuster Drugs Finance Innovation

To understand why, you need to take a look inside the machinery of pharmaceutical innovation and understand the genesis of medical breakthroughs.

Major pharmaceutical companies are built upon and driven by blockbuster drugs. At this point, that's defined as a product with sales of above a billion dollars a year. All the "Big Pharma" companies have some of these very big drugs anchoring their portfolios, and most have grown by developing or acquiring a series of them over the years.

Blockbusters tend to be highly innovative drugs, often breakthroughs. They are big because they represent the first or best treatment for a major medical need. At the same time, they are very elusive, very rare. No company has ever found a way to produce big, innovative drugs efficiently, economically, or even predictably. For all its technological sophistication, the business model centered on innovation is pretty primitive.

As long as we can continue to find some big new drugs, we can afford to bring . . . lesser ones to market as well.

Think of a funnel, with the wide end representing the discovery stage and the narrow end representing the launch point of a new product. Thousands of compounds enter the top of the funnel and begin to undergo testing. A large percentage fail very early. More fail at each stage of development. But ultimately a few do make it through. You've probably seen the attrition statistics before—for every 5,000 entering the top, one comes out the bottom. This is part of the reason why it costs $800 million to $1 billion to produce a new drug.

Of those that make it to market, not all are big drugs by any means. In fact, only one in three makes back its cost of development. So the true blockbusters are a fraction of the fraction that survives the journey. And yet these few throw off enough value to make the innovation model work. Among other benefits, they pay for all the failures, but also for the lesser innovation that occurs along the way. These discoveries may have smaller markets and thus represent lower return to the companies. But they are critically important to those who suffer from these diseases, and, as long as we can continue to find some big new drugs, we can afford to bring these lesser ones to market as well.

Most importantly, blockbusters finance the search for more breakthroughs, which makes our innovation engine run something like a breeder reactor, the nuclear energy system that produces fuel even as it consumes fuel.

This is not simply a matter of having the resources to re-load the top of the funnel. Rather the key resources are those required to keep moving a "critical mass" of compounds through the R&D funnel. It's the "D" that's rate limiting, not the "R."

High Cost of Technological Risk

This is a key to understanding where innovation comes from, so let me take it one layer deeper.

Think of the funnel again. Superimposed over the funnel of scientific attrition, there is an inverse funnel of cash out-lays, a stream that gets wider and wider as the molecules move forward. It's well known that the greatest expense occurs in the third and final phase of clinical trials and so this is the part of the innovation process that most people associate with the capabilities of the big companies. But there is an earlier, less visible stage of development that I would say really de-fines the engine room in the innovation machine.

This is the period between candidate selection, where one molecule is selected for further development from a "family" of kindred compounds, and the stage where a surviving drug candidate is tested for efficacy in patients, which is the begin-ning of Phase II clinical trials. In between, the candidate is tested for toxicity and for all sorts of other properties that de-termine whether it can be moved into human beings and, ul-timately, commercialized as a marketable product.

The key thing about this part of drug development is that it combines high costs with high technological risk. Moving a compound from candidate selection through first human dose involves a lot of people putting in a lot of hours in many dis-ciplines. By the time you reach the end of Phase I, you may have $100 million invested in that compound when you in-clude the cost of all failures and the cost of capital. Yet 70 percent of the molecules that make it this far will never make it to market, and none of this work tells you what you most want to know—will it work?

But you have to be willing and able to place your bets despite the uncertainty. Your chances of succeeding are improved by having a lot of candidates to move forward. But bringing a lot of candidates forward means proportionally greater expenditures. Unless you have one or more big drugs on the market to give you these resources, you just can't afford the risks that go with a sustained pursuit of innovation.

Incidentally, this explains why the vast majority of new drugs come from pharmaceutical companies and not from university or government labs. That claim has been advanced in several recent attacks on the industry, but it is simply not true. These scientists can do the early part of the "R," and in fact they do contribute a lot of new ideas for the top of the funnel. But they are simply not staffed, funded, or organized to do the "D." The capabilities really don't exist outside the industry. Even smaller pharmaceutical companies and most biotechs typically partner with the major companies to bring their molecules through the development process.

Obviously, this business of finding significant new pharmaceutical treatments is a very high risk proposition. The only thing that induces people to put their money and their time and talents into it is the prospect of a return commensurate with the risks.

Nobody, under any circumstances, is ever guaranteed that such a return will be achieved. But what guarantees that such a return is possible are the two key principles I noted in my opening: intellectual property protection and market-based pricing. The patent system gives inventors a period of exclusivity in which to try to get their return. Market-based pricing allows successful innovators to actually achieve the level of return their investors require.

Price Controls Would Reduce R&D

The question our policymakers need to ponder is what happens to biomedical research and development if those two principles are compromised to any significant degree? What changes in the model I've described, if we get price controls in "the last free market"?

I believe pharmaceutical companies would focus first on how to survive and later on how to succeed in the new environment. I think the first thing they'd do is to focus much more attention and resources on maximizing sales of existing products. That means much greater marketing spent to try to gain market share, and the only place that money can come from is the research budget.

As the importance of marketing grows, the number of marketers would shrink in an intense wave of consolidation. Many would have no choice but to combine operations and cut costs. But even relatively successful companies would see consolidation as a key strategy for gaining leverage to counter the greater power of the government buyers.

The terrible irony of the campaign against innovation is that it is coming at precisely the moment in history that medicine is poised for a great leap forward.

The net result would be that the industry's total R&D effort would shrink tremendously. Instead of 20 or so medium-to-large companies spending $30 billion a year on research, you might have 4 or 5 huge conglomerates spending half or one-quarter of that amount.

Furthermore, whatever the total amount spent on R&D, it would be allocated much differently than it is today. In the aftermath of new controls, companies would shift resources away from early stage R&D and focus them on developing new indications or line extensions for existing products and on trying to accelerate development of late-stage molecules.

Those are the potential new products that you know the most about and that can come to market soonest. They may be the last new products you'll ever see so you'd better get everything out of them you possibly can.

Then, over time, I think a number of other strategies would emerge to try to offset the lower potential returns by pursuing lower risk ventures. I suspect the dominant strategy would center on deliberate imitation and incremental improvements to existing products. The pharmaceutical market would become a world of "me-toos." There are already quite a few companies that haven't been successful at innovation and so already depend heavily on this kind of incrementalism. Ironically, they might actually have an advantage in the new world. . . .

Innovation Is Needed to Defeat Disease

So again, I put it to you—do you believe we already have all the innovation we need? In the very near future you are going to have a chance to give your answer, and your answer is going to count.

As health care costs continue to rise, as our society tries to cope with the retirement of 76 million baby boomers, I'm sure there will be some voices willing to argue in the affirmative.

We need to understand, once and for all, that innovation is not the problem. It is the solution.

For the other side, we must imagine the voices of all who suffer from illnesses we cannot yet defeat: the millions who suffer from heart failure, from Alzheimer's, from a dozen deadly cancers, from the complications of diabetes, and on and on. How do they vote?

The terrible irony of the campaign against innovation is that it is coming at precisely the moment in history that medicine is poised for a great leap forward.

For all our amazing advances in the last 50 years, we are still working with the tools of the first pharmaceutical revolution. That is, we are still mostly using advanced chemistry to treat disease symptoms. In the new age we are now entering, we will increasingly use advanced biology to actually cure or even prevent disease from occurring.

The fruits of genomics and other new disciplines in biomedicine will clearly take some time, longer than we first thought, to transform therapeutics. But that transformation will come if we do not interdict it with short-sighted controls. To do that would forsake millions of sufferers and yet never deliver effective cost control. It would leave us stranded part way along the curve of progress—advanced enough to do some good at great cost but not enough to really begin to shrink the massive cost of disease.

We need to understand, once and for all, that innovation is not the problem. It is the solution.

Controlling Drug Prices Would Reduce Access to Medicine

Doug Bandow

Doug Bandow was a senior fellow at the Cato Institute at the time this viewpoint was written. He is currently a vice president of Citizen Outreach and the author of several books.

The Food and Drug Administration has approved a drug to combat non-Hodgkin's lymphoma. That's good news for cancer patients in America and around the world. But you wouldn't know it, given the vicious political campaign being directed against the pharmaceutical industry.

America's drugmakers are under attack. Congressmen are pushing to cut prices and trim patent rights.... State legislators are debating their own draconian price control schemes. The media, such as the PBS show *Frontline*, has targeted the drugmakers. Trial attorneys, left-wing activists, and state attorneys general are filing lawsuits charging pharmaceutical firms with everything from racketeering to fraud.

This assault is not new. Drug companies have been under pressure for a decade. When the [Bill] Clinton administration attempted to nationalize American health care, it sought to demonize the drugmakers as well as most doctors and hospitals.

Unfortunately, years of demagoguery advanced for political profit are having an impact. Public opinions of the industry have been falling sharply. While Americans have yet to agree with [former vice president] Al Gore's grotesque comparison of the drugmakers to the tobacco companies and "big polluters" ... they are increasingly turning on an industry that

Doug Bandow "Healers Under Siege," *National Review*, July 11, 2003. www.nationalreview.com. Reproduced by permission.

has done so much to improve their lives. [Poll takers] Harris-Interactive reports that those who believe the drugmakers are doing a good job of serving consumers fell from 79 percent to 57 percent from just 1997 to 2001.

New Drugs Are Saving Lives

Yet new pharmaceuticals are responsible for almost half of the reduced mortality among different diseases between 1970 and 1991. Columbia University's Frank Lichtenberg figures that every new drug approved during that time saves over 11,000 life-years annually. And the benefits continue. He estimates that fully 40 percent of the increase in average lifespan between 1986 and 2000 is due to new drugs.

"Three decades ago medical technology was rather primitive by today's standards," says Dr. E. M. Kolassa of the University of Mississippi School of Pharmacy. "Today, physicians have at their disposal medications and technologies that provide for the immediate diagnosis and treatment of most of the disorders that affect modern man."

Hundreds of new drugs are in development for cancer, heart disease, strokes, Alzheimer's, infectious diseases, and AIDS. Consider the latter: Two decades ago there was no treatment for AIDS. By 1987 there was one drug, AZT. Now there are 74 anti-AIDS drugs available and another 100 in development.

[Other countries'] ill citizens have far less access to important medications. . . . Patients often wait years for life-saving products.

Similarly, pharmaceuticals offer the best hope of combating any future outbreak of SARS [severe acute respiratory syndrome], which has killed over 700 people. In fact, the quickest solution is to find an existing medicine that works. Laboratories are currently screening some 2000 approved and experimental drugs to see if they are useful in fighting SARS.

Yeoh Eng-kiong, Hong Kong's secretary of health, welfare, and food, observes that not treating the sick isn't an option: "Under such desperate situations, you try your best." And that means experimenting. Gurinder Shahi, a doctor in Singapore, explains: "Given how little we know about SARS and the reality that it is killing people, it is justified for us to be daring and innovative in coming up with solutions."

Daring innovation is most likely to come in a competitive, profit-driven market. After all, today's medicines exist only because there is a bevy of sophisticated pharmaceutical companies devoted to finding drugs to heal the sick.

Isn't this serving consumers well?

Prices Must Cover Costs

Ah, but prices are high. Too high, in the view of myopic, vote-seeking politicians. "There's no question that prescription drugs cost too much in this nation," claims Sen. Jim Jeffords (I., Vt.).

Why, yes. They only save lives. Extend our life spans. Moderate our pain. Control our nausea. Eliminate our need for surgery. Treat our allergies.

Why should we have to pay for such products? The outrage. The horror. Drugs should be free. Or at least a lot cheaper.

Every attempt to stop people from using new medicines endangers their health and threatens to increase health costs elsewhere.

It would be nice if they were, of course, but people who believe prices can be lowered legislatively are living in the world as it ought to be. Everyone ought to be rich and beautiful. Everyone out to be paid a million dollars a year for working ten hours a week.

Everyone ought to have a Mercedes at a Yugo price. Everyone ought to have a mansion for the price of a shack. And everyone ought to have all of the pharmaceuticals now available, but for less money.

Life as it ought to be.

Unfortunately, pharmaceuticals do not appear outside company doors every morning like manna from heaven appeared in the Promised Land for the ancient Israelites. Instead, firms review numerous plausible substances: of every 5,000 to 10,000 checked, 250 make it to animal testing. About five reach human trials. Only one gets past the Food and Drug Administration (FDA) onto the market. That one has to pay for the research costs of the other 5,000 to 10,000. It ain't easy.

Thus, the real cost of pharmaceuticals is not making the pill that patients swallow. It's the research that went into developing the pill—as well as the other 9,999 substances that never made it to the market. The pill's price also has to cover the cost of running the company and complying with burdensome FDA requirements.

The Tufts Center for the Study of Drug Development estimates that companies spend nearly $900 million over a ten- or fifteen-year period to develop each drug. America's major research firms alone spent $32 billion on R&D [research & development][in 2002].

Price Controls Mean Less Access to Drugs

Nevertheless, some politicians would control prices directly. For instance, legislators in Maine want to impose rates that they think are fair and are threatening retaliation if any company tries to pull out of the market in response. Washington already demands super-discounts for some of its programs.

But government can only confiscate the drugmakers' existing inventory. It can't force them to keep making drugs to be confiscated in the future.

Adopting Canadian- or European-style controls will result in a Canadian- or European-style drug industry and patient access. These countries do their best to free ride off of America, but their pharmaceutical industries are weak and getting weaker.

Moreover, their ill citizens have far less access to important medications. The group Europe Economics warns that patients often wait years for life-saving products.

Still, America's political air is filled with other alleged panaceas [cure-alls]. Reimportation from Canada is pushed even by some conservatives. Yet prices are lower there because the government imposes price controls and litigation costs are less—the country is not full of profit-minded tort attorneys. Charging Canadian (or Mexican, or Afghan) prices in the U.S. means the drugs would not be developed in the first place.

Increased use of generics is another idea. Generics are an important component of the existing market, accounting for almost half of all prescriptions written. But generics companies provide very little independent R&D to develop new products, the lifeblood of medical progress.

Politicians also are pushing a range of utilization restrictions—formularies, reference pricing, and more. Yet every attempt to stop people from using new medicines endangers their health and threatens to increase health costs elsewhere. For instance, Frank Lichtenberg estimates that replacing 1000 older prescriptions with newer drugs raises pharmaceutical costs by $18,000 but cuts hospital costs by $44,000.

Everyone in America has a stake in lowering health-care costs. But they also have a stake in maintaining quality health care. If the pharmaceutical industry succumbs to the demagogic campaign against it, we will all suffer the painful consequences.

CHAPTER 4

Are Dishonest or Illegal Prescription Drug Practices Common?

Chapter Preface

Prescription drugs have become such a major part of today's economy, and of ordinary people's lives, that they now give rise to many problems besides the basic question of whether particular ones are safe, effective, affordable, or appropriate. Among these problems is the growth of dishonest or illegal activities.

For example, health-care experts are concerned because pharmaceutical companies influence the prescribing habits of doctors, not through overt bribery but in more subtle ways, such as distributing reprints of biased articles from medical journals and financing continuing education. Conferences attended by influential doctors are arranged by drug companies and are often held in luxurious surroundings. Dr. John Abramson, author of *Overdo$ed America*, writes, "I've turned down more offers than I can count for 'educational' dinners, sporting events, golf and ski outings, and even weekends in the best hotels plus $500."

It is not that doctors prescribe new drugs without being convinced of their effectiveness. On the contrary, most of them believe what they read or are told by medical authorities, and much of it is true. Nevertheless, when they are given only the favorable information about a certain drug, they cannot judge it objectively without having observed the long-term reactions of their patients. Also, the pharmaceutical companies often provide them with free samples. This practice helps patients who cannot afford expensive drugs, so doctors generally consider it a good thing. Some observers doubt its benefits, however, because the sample drug may not be any better than cheaper ones and may not be necessary at all— and the doctor may go on prescribing it merely because doing so has become familiar. Therefore, the practice of providing such samples is being questioned.

A more evident problem is that prescription drugs can be obtained without prescriptions on the Internet, although such sales are against the law. This practice can lead to serious harm even when the drugs so obtained are genuine, though sometimes they are not. Some people who buy these drugs have had prescriptions for them in the past and are simply trying to avoid the expense of another doctor's visit, but others are experimenting with drugs that they have merely heard about and that may not be appropriate for them. Not only is it likely that such self-medication will not help them, but it may prevent them from seeking treatment—or worse, may have damaging effects.

Furthermore, young people have begun to obtain prescription drugs on the Internet for getting high, in the mistaken belief that these drugs are safer than street drugs. Abuse of prescription drugs is increasing much faster than the use of illegal drugs. Medical authorities and law enforcement officials all agree that this is dangerous, but so far they have struggled unsuccessfully to put an end to it.

Even when people have a legitimate need for drugs, if they buy them without prescriptions they cannot be sure of getting what they believe they are getting. And unfortunately, counterfeit drugs are not confined to those illegally obtained. Since there is big money in counterfeiting expensive medications, criminals have found ways to distribute them to wholesalers that supply innocent pharmacies. A patient may unknowingly receive a contaminated drug or a diluted one or a totally inactive substance; at best, that person's illness will be untreated, while at worst the substitution may result in death.

The topics addressed in this chapter pose significant problems for consumers, physicians, and pharmaceutical companies, and most agree that the solutions will not be easily found.

Gifts from Pharmaceutical Companies Influence Doctors

Adriane Fugh-Berman and Shahram Ahari

Adriane Fugh-Berman is an associate professor at Georgetown Medical Center in Washington, D.C. Shahram Ahari is a former pharmaceutical sales representative now with the University of California School of Pharmacy in San Francisco.

In 2000, pharmaceutical companies spent more than 15.7 billion dollars on promoting prescription drugs in the United States. More than 4.8 billion dollars was spent on detailing, the one-on-one promotion of drugs to doctors by pharmaceutical sales representatives, commonly called drug reps. The average sales force expenditure for pharmaceutical companies is $875 million annually.

Unlike the door-to-door vendors of cosmetics and vacuum cleaners, drug reps do not sell their product directly to buyers. Consumers pay for prescription drugs, but physicians control access. Drug reps increase drug sales by influencing physicians, and they do so with finely titrated doses of friendship. This article, which grew out of conversations between a former drug rep (Shahram Ahari) and a physician who researches pharmaceutical marketing (Adriane Fugh-Berman), reveals the strategies used by reps to manipulate physician prescribing.

Better than You Know Yourself

Reps may be genuinely friendly, but they are not genuine friends. Drug reps are selected for their presentability and outgoing natures, and are trained to be observant, personable, and helpful. They are also trained to assess physicians' personalities, practice styles, and preferences, and to relay this infor-

Adriane Fugh-Berman and Shahram Ahari, "Following the Script: How Drug Reps Make Friends and Influence Doctors," *PLoS Medicine*, April 24, 2007. www.pubmed central.nih.gov. Reproduced by permission.

mation back to the company. Personal information may be more important than prescribing preferences. Reps ask for and remember details about a physician's family life, professional interests, and recreational pursuits. A photo on a desk presents an opportunity to inquire about family members and memorize whatever tidbits are offered (including names, birthdays, and interests); these are usually typed into a database after the encounter. Reps scour a doctor's office for objects—a tennis racquet, Russian novels, seventies rock music, fashion magazines, travel mementos, or cultural or religious symbols—that can be used to establish a personal connection with the doctor.

Good details are dynamic; the best reps tailor their messages constantly according to their client's reaction. A friendly physician makes the rep's job easy, because the rep can use the "friendship" to request favors, in the form of prescriptions. Physicians who view the relationship as a straightforward goods-for-prescriptions exchange are dealt with in a business-like manner. Skeptical doctors who favor evidence over charm are approached respectfully, supplied with reprints from the medical literature, and wooed as teachers. Physicians who refuse to see reps are detailed by proxy; their staff is dined and flattered in hopes that they will act as emissaries for a rep's messages.

Physicians invited and paid by a rep to speak to their peers may express their gratitude in increased prescriptions.

Gifts create both expectation and obligation. "The importance of developing loyalty through gifting cannot be overstated," writes Michael Oldani, an anthropologist and former drug rep. Pharmaceutical gifting, however, involves carefully calibrated generosity. Many prescribers receive pens, notepads, and coffee mugs, all items kept close at hand, ensuring that a targeted drug's name stays uppermost in a physician's subconscious mind. High prescribers receive higher-end presents, for example, silk ties or golf bags. As Oldani states, "The essence of pharmaceutical gifting . . . is 'bribes that aren't considered bribes'".

Reps also recruit and audition "thought leaders" (physicians respected by their peers) to groom for the speaking circuit. Physicians invited and paid by a rep to speak to their peers may express their gratitude in increased prescriptions. Anything that improves the relationship between the rep and the client usually leads to improved market share.

Script Tracking

Pharmaceutical companies monitor the return on investment of detailing—and all promotional efforts—by prescription tracking. Information distribution companies, also called health information organizations (including IMS Health, Dendrite, Verispan, and Wolters Kluwer), purchase prescription records from pharmacies. The majority of pharmacies sell these records; IMS Health, the largest information distribution company, procures records on about 70% of prescriptions filled in community pharmacies. Patient names are not included, and physicians may be identified only by state license number, Drug Enforcement Administration number, or a pharmacy-specific identifier. Data that identify physicians only by numbers are linked to physician names through licensing agreements with the American Medical Association (AMA), which maintains the Physician Masterfile, a database containing demographic information on all US physicians (living or dead, member or non-member, licensed or non-licensed). In 2005, database product sales, including an unknown amount from licensing Masterfile information, provided more than $44 million to the AMA.

Pharmaceutical companies are the primary customers for prescribing data, which are used both to identify "high-prescribers" and to track the effects of promotion. Physicians are ranked on a scale from one to ten based on how many prescriptions they write. Reps lavish high-prescribers with attention, gifts, and unrestricted "educational" grants. Cardiologists and other specialists write relatively few prescriptions, but are targeted because specialist prescriptions are perpetuated for years by primary care physicians, thus affecting market share.

Reps use prescribing data to see how many of a physician's patients receive specific drugs, how many prescriptions the physician writes for targeted and competing drugs, and how a physician's prescribing habits change over time. One training guide states that an "individual market share report for each physician . . . pinpoints a prescriber's current habits" and is "used to identify which products are currently in favor with the physician in order to develop a strategy to change those prescriptions into Merck prescriptions."

A *Pharmaceutical Executive* article states, "A physician's prescribing value is a function of the opportunity to prescribe, plus his or her attitude toward prescribing, along with outside influences. By building these multiple dimensions into physicians' profiles, it is possible to understand the 'why' behind the 'what' and 'how' of their behavior." To this end, some companies combine data sources. For example, Medical Marketing Service "enhances the AMA Masterfile with non-AMA data from a variety of sources to not only include demographic selections, but also behavioral and psychographic selections that help you to better target your perfect prospects."

The goal of this demographic slicing and dicing is to identify physicians who are most susceptible to marketing efforts. One industry article suggests categorizing physicians as "hidden gems": "Initially considered 'low value' because they are low prescribers, these physicians can change their prescribing habits after targeted, effective marketing." "Growers" are "Physicians who are early adopters of a brand. Pharmaceutical companies employ retention strategies to continue to reinforce their growth behavior." Physicians are considered "low value" "due to low category share and prescribing level".

In an interview with *Pharmaceutical Representative*, Fred Marshall, president of Quantum Learning, explained, ". . . One type might be called 'the spreader' who uses a little bit of everybody's product. The second type might be a 'loyalist', who's very loyal to one particular product and uses it for most patient types. Another physician might be a 'niche' physician, who reserves our product only for a very narrowly defined patient type. And the idea in physician segmentation would be to have a different messaging strategy for each of those physician segments".

In *Pharmaceutical Executive*, Ron Brand of IMS Consulting writes ". . . integrated segmentation analyzes individual prescribing behaviors, demographics, and psychographics (attitudes, beliefs, and values) to fine-tune sales targets. For a particular product, for example, one segment might consist of price-sensitive physicians, another might include doctors loyal to a given manufacturers brand, and a third may include those unfriendly towards reps".

The purpose of supplying drug samples is to gain entry into doctors' offices, and to habituate physicians to prescribing targeted drugs.

In recent years, physicians have become aware of—and dismayed by—script tracking. In July 2006, the AMA launched the Prescribing Data Restriction Program, which allows physicians the opportunity to withhold most prescribing information from reps and their supervisors (anyone above that level, however, has full access to all data). According to an article in *Pharmaceutical Executive*, "Reps and direct managers can view the physician's prescribing volume quantiled at the therapeutic class level" and can still view aggregated or segmented data including "categories into which the prescriber falls, such as an early-adopter of drugs, for example. . . ." The pharmaceutical industry supports the Prescribing Data Restriction Program, which is seen as a less onerous alternative to, for example, state legislation passed in New Hampshire forbidding the sale of prescription data to commercial entities.

The Value of Samples

The purpose of supplying drug samples is to gain entry into doctors' offices, and to habituate physicians to prescribing targeted drugs. Physicians appreciate samples, which can be used to start therapy immediately, test tolerance to a new drug, or reduce the total cost of a prescription. Even physicians who refuse to see drug reps usually want samples (these docs are denigrated as "sample-grabbers"). Patients like samples too; it's nice to get a little present from the doctor. Samples also double as unacknowledged gifts to physicians and their staff. The convenience of an in-house pharmacy increases loyalty to both the reps and the drugs they represent.

Some physicians use samples to provide drugs to indigent patients. Using samples for an entire course of treatment is anathema to pharmaceutical companies because this "cannibalizes" sales. Among the aims of one industry sample-tracking program are to "reallocate samples to high-opportunity prescribers most receptive to sampling as a promotional vehicle" and "identify prescribers who were oversampled and take corrective action immediately".

Studies consistently show that samples influence prescribing choices. Reps provide samples only of the most promoted, usually most expensive, drugs, and patients given a sample for part of a course of treatment almost always receive a prescription for the same drug.

Funding Friendship

Drug costs now account for 10.7% of health-care expenditures in the US. In 2004, spending for prescription drugs was $188.5

billion, almost five times as much as what was spent in 1990. Between 1995 and 2005, the number of drug reps in the US increased from 38,000 to 100,000—about one for every six physicians. The actual ratio is close to one drug rep per 2.5 targeted doctors, because not all physicians practice, and not all practicing physicians are detailed. Low-prescribers are ignored by drug reps.

Physicians view drug information provided by reps as a convenient, if not entirely reliable, educational service. An industry survey found that more than half of "high-prescribing" doctors cited drug reps as their main source of information about new drugs. In another study, three quarters of 2,608 practicing physicians found information provided by reps "very useful" (15%) or "somewhat useful" (59%). However, only 9% agreed that the information was "very accurate"; 72% thought the information was "somewhat accurate"; and 14% said that it was "not very" or "not at all" accurate.

Physicians are susceptible to corporate influence because they are overworked, overwhelmed with information and paperwork, and feel underappreciated.

Whether or not physicians believe in the accuracy of information provided, detailing is extremely effective at changing prescribing behavior, which is why it is worth its substantial expense. The average annual income for a drug rep is $81,700, which includes $62,400 in base salary plus $19,300 in bonuses. The average cost of recruiting, hiring, and training a new rep is estimated to be $89,000. When expenses are added to income and training, pharmaceutical companies spend $150,000 annually per primary care sales representative and $330,000 per specialty sales representative. An industry article states, "The pharmaceutical industry averages $31.9 million in annual sales spending per primary-care drug. . . . Sales spending for specialty drugs that treat a narrowed population segment average $25.3 million per product across the industry."

Calculated Kindness

As one of us (Shahram Ahari) explained in testimony in the litigation over New Hampshire's new ban on the commercial sale of prescription data, the concept that reps provide necessary services to physicians and patients is a fiction. Pharmaceutical companies spend billions of dollars annually to ensure that physicians most susceptible to marketing prescribe the most expensive, most promoted drugs to the most people possible. The foundation of this influence is a sales force of 100,000 drug reps that provides rationed doses of samples, gifts, services, and flattery to a subset of physicians. If detailing were an educational service, it would be provided to all physicians, not just those who affect market share.

Physicians are susceptible to corporate influence because they are overworked, overwhelmed with information and paperwork, and feel underappreciated. Cheerful and charming, bearing food and gifts, drug reps provide respite and sympathy; they appreciate how hard doctors' lives are, and seem only to want to ease their burdens. But, as Shahram Ahari's New Hampshire testimony reflects, every word, every courtesy, every gift, and every piece of information provided is carefully crafted, not to assist doctors or patients, but to increase market share for targeted drugs. In the interests of patients, physicians must reject the false friendship provided by reps. Physicians must rely on information on drugs from unconflicted sources, and seek friends among those who are not paid to be friends.

Media Reporting About Prescription Drugs Is Often Inaccurate

Richard A. Deyo and Donald L. Patrick

Richard A. Deyo is Kaiser Permanente Professor of Evidence-Based Family Medicine at Oregon Health and Science University in Portland, and Donald L. Patrick is a professor of health policy at the University of Washington in Seattle.

Reporting on new drugs, in particular, is common enough that it's been possible to study the characteristics of these reports. Ray Moynihan, an Australian broadcast journalist who has spent time studying in the United States, teamed with Lisa Bero, a pharmacologist at the University of California, San Francisco, and some colleagues to analyze 180 newspaper articles and 27 television reports concerning three drugs. They studied two drugs that were new and still on patent: Pravachol for lowering cholesterol and Fosamax for osteoporosis. The third drug was an old off-patent drug, aspirin for preventing heart disease.

Common Reporting Pitfalls

Less than half the reports they studied mentioned side effects of the drugs, and only 30 percent mentioned cost. There were 85 stories among the 207 that cited an expert who had ties to drug manufacturers, but only 39 percent of the press reports mentioned this conflict of interest. While reports typically indicated that a drug was effective, only 60 percent indicated just how effective. In the vast majority of cases, only *relative* benefit was reported, not the *absolute* benefit. An example illustrates why this distinction is important.

On the same day in 1996, ABC, CBS, and NBC all carried stories about Fosamax, in response to a conference that had reported a major new study. All three networks reported that the osteoporosis drug reduced the risk of hip fractures by 50 percent, which one reporter described as "almost miraculous." This was the *relative* risk reduction. None reported the *absolute* risk of fracture, which was 2 percent in untreated women and 1 percent in treated women. Going from 2 percent to 1 percent is a 50 percent relative reduction, of course, but many viewers would find the 1 percent absolute difference in risk less impressive. Only one story mentioned abdominal distress as a side effect; and none mentioned that the research had been funded by the drug maker.

In another example of the importance of relative versus absolute risk reduction, Marcia Angell, then editor of the *New England Journal of Medicine*, described a study showing that women who drink alcohol have a 30 percent relative increase in breast cancer risk over ten years. That sounds like a big risk, and if you multiply it times the whole U.S. population, it may be important. But for an individual middle-aged woman with a ten-year breast cancer risk of about 3 percent, a 30 percent relative increase would mean that her absolute risk would rise to 4 percent. In other words, her chance of remaining cancer-free drops from 97 percent to 96 percent. Says Angell, "Is that worth giving up your dinner wine for? Probably not."

It would be unthinkable to leave the sports or financial page in the hands of someone who was unfamiliar with the field, but when it comes to medical reporting . . . inexperience is the norm.

Another common pitfall in reporting is the seduction of surrogate outcomes. When a treatment lowers cholesterol, shrinks tumors, or abolishes abnormal heart rhythms, it's easy to assume that it improves longevity. However, a long and growing list of counterexamples makes it important to focus on the outcome that is of real interest. Drugs that lower cholesterol or normalize heart rhythm have sometimes paradoxically increased mortality, and tumor shrinkage is a notoriously poor indicator of real benefit. Doctors and researchers, as well as journalists, are often seduced by these surrogate outcomes, making the reporter's job more difficult.

Of course, another problem is simply erroneous reporting. A study from the Loma Linda VA Medical Center and School of Medicine examined 587 articles from major newspapers and magazines, using two independent evaluators. They reported misleading and serious errors in 32 percent of press reports. . . . Again, the blame for these errors may be shared by journalists and researchers.

Misleading Anecdotes

Another pitfall in medical reporting involves the use of human interest stories. To a scientist, a single person's story is an anecdote, just one piece of data in a much larger body of information. Long-term results and typical results for an average patient may be obscured by the anecdotal case. For journalists, however, stories about individual patients make a news report interesting and may help to give the audience a vicarious sense of a disease or treatment. If the story is representative of typical cases, it can be informative, but if it's exceptional, it may mislead.

Doctors or commercial interests sometimes exaggerate or overmedicalize problems because it suits their purposes.

An example of misleading anecdotes comes from University of Washington researchers, headed by Dr. Wylie Burke, an internist and chair of the Department of Medical History and

Ethics. Burke and her colleagues studied reports on breast cancer in popular magazines, examining 172 individual vignettes. Of these, 47 percent described women with breast cancer discovered before age forty. In reality, only 3.6 percent of all breast cancer cases occur among women this age.

There's a chance that this sort of reporting might actually lead to adverse health outcomes. Burke and her colleagues noted that these stories misrepresent the age distribution of breast cancer, emphasizing atypical cases. Their concern was that this contributed to young women's fears of breast cancer and overestimates of risk. In turn, they noted that such fears may lead young women to overestimate the value of mammography before age fifty or of prevention with the drug tamoxifen. For older women, such reporting might obscure the fact that risk increases with age, reducing the motivation for appropriate mammography screening.

Yet another common error is to mistake an association for causality. For example, if a researcher found that people with lung cancer were more likely to drink alcohol than people without lung cancer, it might be tempting to assume that alcohol causes lung cancer. But this would be wrong. It's just that cigarette smokers are more likely to drink alcohol than non-smokers, and it's the cigarettes that create the risk.

In some cases, diseases have virtually been invented to help market drugs.

Doctors, of course, sometimes make the same mistake. When they observed that women who were taking hormone replacement therapy had fewer heart attacks than those who weren't, many assumed that the hormone replacement prevented heart disease. The technology seemed to work. Only when randomized trials showed a contrary result did it become clear that healthier women were more likely to take hormone replacement—and that was the reason for their lower risk of heart disease, not the hormones. So both medics and the media need to be more sophisticated in making inferences about cause and effect.

The organization and habits of health journalism sometimes contribute to poor reporting. Reporters often feel a "need for speed," to get developments into print as quickly as possible. This approach can be diametrically opposed to the need for context, a sense of incremental progress, and the scientific view that a single study is rarely definitive.

Finally, in many local newspapers and television stations, health stories are assigned to reporters with little medical knowledge. It would be unthinkable to leave the sports or financial page in the hands of someone who was unfamiliar with the field, but when it comes to medical reporting, which can directly affect people's health, inexperience is the norm. This is less a problem with national networks or newspapers like the *New York Times* and the *Wall Street Journal*, but is often a major concern with local outlets.

In some cases, [news accounts] fail to note that patients may have an excellent prognosis without treatment at all.

Disease Mongering

Sometimes the media distort the magnitude or the severity of a medical problem, or fail to note that it can often be self-limiting. How many stories on back pain, for example, point out that the vast majority of cases get better on their own? Some stories confidently report on the staggering human toll of conditions such as chronic Lyme disease, premenstrual dysphoric syndrome, or multiple chemical sensitivity—conditions that have no agreed-upon criteria or definitions, and that remain controversial within the medical community. We don't mean to minimize the suffering of patients who receive these diagnoses, but the ambiguity of the conditions' definitions and meanings is sometimes lost in press accounts. Catastrophic illnesses are always more newsworthy than symptoms.

Of course, doctors or commercial interests sometimes exaggerate or overmedicalize problems because it suits their purposes. Irritable bowel syndrome has long been identified as a generally mild condition with no precise criteria: It's often a "diagnosis of exclusion" when testing shows no other cause for persistent symptoms of abdominal cramping, diarrhea, or constipation. But when GlaxoSmithKline was preparing to market its new drug for irritable bowel syndrome, Lotronex, it described irritable bowel syndrome as affecting up to 20 percent of the population and posing a large burden of illness. Other estimates are that the syndrome occurs in about 5 percent of the population, and severely affects only 5 percent of those.

The drug company hired a PR [public relations] firm to mount a three-year "education program" to create a new perception of irritable bowel syndrome as a "serious, credible, common, and concrete" disease. The goal was to shape medical and public opinion about the condition. A leaked document indicated that "PR and media activities are crucial to a well-rounded campaign—particularly in the area of consumer awareness." A marketing magazine noted that key objectives in the period prior to drug approval were to "establish a need" for a new drug and to "create the desire" among doctors who write the prescriptions. The manufacturer marketed the drug, but then recalled it for severe side effects and deaths. The company then pressured the FDA [U.S. Food and Drug Administration] to allow remarketing, though with new restrictions.

In some cases, diseases have virtually been invented to help market drugs. "Social phobia" was not a diagnosis recognized by doctors, but it was used effectively as a way to expand the market for new antidepressant drugs. The manufacturers issued press releases, some of them picked up by the media, describing the severe impact of the "disease" and its high prevalence.

On the flip side, companies sometimes exaggerate the side effects of a competitor's treatment to emphasize the putative advantages of their own. Perhaps this should be labeled "complication mongering." In any event, both reporters and readers need to be alert to the potential for disease mongering as they consider health news. Journalists should routinely question (and preferably avoid) corporate-sponsored material on the prevalence or impact of a disease.

Sometimes, with encouragement from manufacturers or researchers, news reports begin long before any scientifically valid data are available.

A related concern is creating the appearance that there's no alternative to some new technology. News accounts often fail to describe older, less expensive treatments that may be equally effective for many patients. In some cases, they fail to note that patients may have an excellent prognosis without treatment at all.

Why Wait for Evidence?

Sometimes, with encouragement from manufacturers or researchers, news reports begin long before any scientifically valid data are available. [Reports] on artificial discs for patients with spine disorders exemplifies the problems. Although artificial discs [were] being developed and evaluated by several manufacturers, they were only reviewed by the FDA in mid-2004. . . . Until 2004, the evidence for their effectiveness had come largely from short-term case series with no comparison group, so the FDA did not regard their safety and efficacy as having been established.

But glowing press reports had already become common. . . .

Preliminary drug reports are often met with similar enthusiasm. Recently, a paper presented at the annual meeting of the American College of Rheumatology, based on just five patients, created a major media stir. One headline reported that the treatment might "cure rheumatoid arthritis," while another announced a "breakthrough as scientists discover the cure for arthritis." This extraordinary response was based on a tiny group of patients who received not only the study drug, but two other drugs simultaneously. Side effects of the combined therapy were rarely mentioned, and follow-up was just eighteen months, for what is ordinarily a lifelong disease. The $4,000 cost for three weeks of therapy went largely unnoticed. A sober observer noted that spectacular results in small, uncontrolled series of rheumatoid arthritis patients were common, but that they often couldn't be reproduced in more stringent controlled trials.

Focus on Access, Not Effectiveness

The problem, of course, is that false hopes are often raised in the public's mind by such reports. In the case of back pain, for example, we have a long track record of false starts and marginally effective treatments. This track record alone should be noted in reports, and should give reporters pause. Rather than acknowledging that many new treatments are unproven, however, press reports often imply that they are being held back by regulatory foot-dragging or reluctant insurance companies. Many stories focus on access to the treatment rather than on its effectiveness.

Indeed, in the era of managed care, reporting on new medical technology rarely noted that experimental treatments were unproven, dangerous, or immensely expensive. If these facts were noted, there was often an implication that ethics dictated that they be ignored. The usual slant was that these treatments were being withheld from needy patients by greedy insurance companies or managed-care companies. These human interest stories, with a David and Goliath conflict, were often irresistible.

The story of high-dose chemotherapy with autologous [recipient-donated] bone marrow transplantation for late-stage breast cancer offered a prime example of such coverage. Even though this treatment fit the description of unproven, toxic, and wildly expensive, breast cancer advocacy groups and others pressed in the early 1990s for its widespread availability. In 1991, *Sixty Minutes* did a story that was highly critical of Aetna's decision not to cover this treatment. In 1993, the media widely publicized a huge jury verdict in favor of California patient Nelene Fox. She had sued her insurance company, Healthnet, for lack of coverage. Similarly, the *Boston Globe* publicized the battle of Charlotte Turner to have her Massachusetts HMO pay for the treatment.

Intense lobbying and public pressure in response to news coverage led the Massachusetts legislature to mandate insurance coverage in 1993. Similar reporting of local cases prompted several other state legislatures to require insurance companies in their states to cover the treatment. Even when laws didn't mandate coverage, most insurance carriers, facing litigation and bad publicity, caved to public demand. When definitive studies were finally reported, it became clear that the fuss was over a treatment that was no more effective than standard therapy, but more toxic, at twice the cost.

Whenever a medical breakthrough is announced, researchers' fame, institutions' reputations, and companies' profits are likely to be at stake.

In retrospect, the media could hardly claim to have protected the public interest. Undoubtedly, many reporters thought they were. Stories of the "little guy" standing up to

Big Business were irresistible. And standing up for "women's rights" may have been particularly attractive. But their failure to distinguish weak from strong evidence contributed to anguish, untoward side effects, and waste of resources that would have been better spent elsewhere. They probably helped to raise insurance premiums for all of us. They were aided and abetted, of course, by zealous but misguided doctors and advocates.

Conveniently Congruent Worldviews

Despite complaints on both sides, the media and medicine may actually share similar worldviews. They generally share an attitude that biotechnology can solve all problems and that medical researchers are heroic. They share a faith in experts and miracle drugs, as well as disdain for evil administrators and bureaucrats. Thus, the media, researchers, industry, and practicing doctors may unconsciously collude to promote an overly favorable view of new medical technology.

Whenever a medical breakthrough is announced, researchers' fame, institutions' reputations, and companies' profits are likely to be at stake. Skepticism by both reporters and the public should be heightened. Joe Palca, of National Public Radio, said, "We could probably ignore 99% of the science news in a given year because its intrinsic value won't be known for many years, or may not be that great." Or as a physician-editorialist suggested, "Hot findings must be handled with care."

Prescription Drugs Are Often Abused

Nichole Aksamit

Nichole Aksamit is a staff writer for the Omaha World-Herald.

An NFL quarterback. A national radio personality. The frontman of a Chicago rock band. . . .

Green Bay Packers quarterback Brett Favre, talk-show host Rush Limbaugh and Wilco singer Jeff Tweedy have battled addiction to narcotics originally prescribed by doctors.

Abuse of Prescription Drugs Is Common

Nationally, an estimated 6.2 million or more Americans abuse prescription drugs. About 1.5 million of them are dependent on prescription painkillers like Vicodin, a popular form of hydrocodone.

In Omaha, Methodist Hospital's emergency department encounters two or three prescription abusers per shift.

Kohll's [an Omaha drug store chain] pharmacists have the Nebraska State Patrol prescription fraud number memorized or close at hand.

Prescription drug abuse often begins innocently, when a doctor prescribes a pain-killer, stimulant or depressant to treat a legitimate health concern.

And an Omaha addiction counselor said roughly one in every five people she treats is hooked on prescription medications.

Pain and addiction experts say prescription drug abuse often begins innocently, when a doctor prescribes a pain-killer, stimulant or depressant to treat a legitimate health concern.

Nichole Aksamit, "Prescription Drugs Can Bring Addiction with Them," *Omaha World-Herald*, July 4, 2004. www.opiates.com. Reproduced by permission.

At first, small doses make you feel better. But the effect decreases as your tolerance builds. You can't afford to miss work or school, so you take extra pills, with or without the doctor's OK.

"It's very easy to justify why you need the next pill," said Dr. Clifford Bernstein, director of the Waismann Institute, a nationally recognized pain clinic and detoxification center in Beverly Hills, Calif. "In your mind, the doctor gave it to you. How bad can it be?"

The relief you got from one Vicodin soon requires two or more. And when you run out of pills, you're in agony because your body is in withdrawal.

A sympathetic doctor gives you more or puts you on 80 mg OxyContin, which packs the punch of about 20 Vicodin.

The more you take, the more you need, and the more you risk overdose. And, of course, the more resources you must spend on getting the drug.

"The clever addict can get any drug he wants just about anytime he wants it," said Rod Colvin, author of *Prescription Drug Addiction: The Hidden Epidemic.*

The former Omaha radio newsman wrote the book after his brother died from complications of a 15-year addiction to anti-anxiety drugs.

Abusers Have Many Ways to Get Drugs

Colvin and others said these are common ways abusers feed their habits:

- Doctor-shopping: Seeing multiple doctors for the same condition to get multiple prescriptions in amounts small enough not to arouse any one doctor's suspicion. This includes complaining of acute pain at various emergency rooms, often at hours when the patient's primary doctor can't be reached.

- Prescription fraud or theft: Stealing the drug or a doctor's Rx pad and forging prescriptions; altering real prescriptions; or phoning in phony ones.

- Using leftovers from friends and relatives or drugs resold on the street.

- Internet shopping. A recent study found nearly 500 Web sites advertising controlled prescription drugs; 94 percent didn't require prescriptions.

Local health-care workers say abusers tend to flock to doctors and pharmacists who are least critical of requests.

"The word gets out, and you've got all these people with addictions at your pharmacy," said David Kohll, co-owner of Kohll's Pharmacies in Omaha. "It's not fun to work there. If their stuff is not ready, they just go crazy."

Often, it's a keen pharmacist who detects the abuser. He or she reports suspicious behavior to the State Patrol, which alerts other pharmacies.

Dr. Mohammad Al-Turk, a family practice physician at Alegent Health's Lakeside Hills clinic [in Omaha], said he rarely prescribes narcotics. When he does, he explains they can be habit-forming and makes patients sign a contract. Patients pledge to take the drugs only as prescribed, not to share them and not to seek additional prescriptions from other doctors—under penalty of being booted from the clinic's care.

Young People Often Trade Prescription Drugs with Friends

Amy Harmon

Amy Harmon is a technology reporter for the New York Times.

Nathan Tylutki arrived late in New York, tired but eager to go out dancing. When his friend Katherine K. offered him the Ritalin she had inherited from someone who had stopped taking his prescription, he popped two pills and stayed out all night.

For the two college friends, now 25 and out in the working world, there was nothing remarkable about the transaction. A few weeks later, Katherine gave the tranquilizer Ativan to another friend who complained of feeling short of breath and panicky. "Clear-cut anxiety disorder," Katherine decreed.

The Ativan came from a former colleague who had traded it to her for the Vicodin that Katherine's boyfriend had been prescribed by a dentist. The boyfriend did not mind, but he preferred that she not give away the Ambien she got from a doctor by exaggerating her sleeping problems. It helps him relax after a stressful day.

It is illegal to give prescription medication to another person, although it is questionable whether the offense would be prosecuted.

"I acquire quite a few medications and then dispense them to my friends as needed. I usually know what I'm talking about," said Katherine, who lives in Manhattan and who, like many other people interviewed for this article, did not want her last name used because of concerns that her behavior could get her in trouble with her employer, law enforcement authorities or at least her parents.

Self-Prescribing Drugs Is Becoming the Norm

For a sizable group of people in their 20's and 30's, deciding on their own what drugs to take—in particular, stimulants, antidepressants and other psychiatric medications—is becoming the norm. Confident of their abilities and often skeptical of psychiatrists' expertise, they choose to rely on their own research and each other's experience in treating problems like depression, fatigue, anxiety or a lack of concentration. A medical degree, in their view, is useful, but not essential, and certainly not sufficient.

They trade unused prescription drugs, get medications without prescriptions from the Internet and, in some cases, lie to doctors to obtain medications that in their judgment they need.

The goal for many young adults is not to get high but to feel better.

A spokeswoman for the Drug Enforcement Administration says it is illegal to give prescription medication to another person, although it is questionable whether the offense would be prosecuted.

The behavior, drug abuse prevention experts say, is notably different from the use of drugs like marijuana or cocaine, or even the abuse of prescription painkillers, which is also on the rise. The goal for many young adults is not to get high but to feel better—less depressed, less stressed out, more focused, better rested. It is just that the easiest route to that end often seems to be medication for which they do not have a prescription.

Some seek to regulate every minor mood fluctuation, some want to enhance their performance at school or work, some simply want to find the best drug to treat a genuine mental illness. And patients say that many general practitioners, pressed for time and unfamiliar with the ever-growing inventory of psychiatric drugs, are happy to take their suggestions, so it pays to be informed.

Doctors and experts in drug abuse . . . say they are flummoxed about how to address the increasing casual misuse of prescription medications by young people.

Health officials say they worry that as prescription pills get passed around in small batches, information about risks and dosage are not included. Even careful self-medicators, they say, may not realize the harmful interaction that drugs can have when used together or may react unpredictably to a drug; Mr. Tylutki and Katherine each had a bad experience with a medication taken without a prescription.

But doctors and experts in drug abuse also say they are flummoxed about how to address the increasing casual misuse of prescription medications by young people for purposes other than getting high.

Carol Boyd, the former head of the Addiction Research Center at the University of Michigan, said medical professionals needed to find ways to evaluate these risks. "Kids get messages about street drugs," Ms. Boyd said. "They know smoking crack is a bad deal. This country needs to have a serious conversation about both the marketing of prescription drugs and where we draw the boundaries between illegal use and misuse."

Better Living Through Chemistry

To some extent, the embrace by young adults of better living through chemistry is driven by familiarity. Unlike previous generations, they have for many years been taking drugs prescribed by doctors for depression, anxiety or attention deficit disorder. Direct-to-consumer drug advertising, approved by the Food and Drug Administration in 1997, has for most of their adult lives sent the message that pills offer a cure for any ill. Which ones to take, many advertisements suggest, is largely a matter of personal choice.

"If a person is having a problem in life, someone who is 42 might not know where to go—'Do I need acupuncture, do I need a new haircut, do I need to read Suze Orman?'" said Casey Greenfield, 32, a writer in Los Angeles, referring to the personal-finance guru. "Someone my age will be like, 'Do I need to switch from Paxil to Prozac?'". . .

Antidepressants are now prescribed to as many as half of the college students seen at student health centers, according to a recent report in the *New England Journal of Medicine*, and increasing numbers of students fake the symptoms of depression or attention disorder to get prescriptions that they believe will give them an edge. Another study, published recently in the *Journal of American College Health*, found that 14 percent of students at a Midwestern liberal arts college reported borrowing or buying prescription stimulants from each other, and that 44 percent knew of someone who had.

"There's this increasingly widespread attitude that 'we are our own best pharmacists,'" said Bessie Oster, the director of "Facts on Tap," a drug abuse prevention program for college students that has begun to focus on prescription drugs. "You'll take something, and if it's not quite right, you'll take a little more or a little less, and there's no notion that you need a doctor to do that."

Going Online for Pills

The new crop of amateur pharmacists varies from those who have gotten prescriptions—after doing their own research and finding a doctor who agreed with them—to those who obtain pills through friends or through some online pharmacies that illegally dispense drugs without prescriptions.

"The mother's little helpers of the 1960's and 1970's are all available now on the Internet," said Catherine Wood, a clinical social worker in Evanston, Ill., who treated one young client who became addicted to Xanax after buying it online. "You don't have to go and steal a prescription pad anymore."

In dozens of interviews, via e-mail and in person, young people spoke of a sense of empowerment that comes from knowing what to prescribe for themselves, or at least where to turn to figure it out. They are as careful with themselves, they say, as any doctor would be with a patient. "It's not like we're passing out Oxycontin, crushing it up and snorting it," said Katherine, who showed a reporter a stockpile that included stimulants, tranquilizers and sleeping pills. "I don't think it's unethical when I have the medication that someone clearly needs to make them feel better to give them a pill or two."

Some say they are increasingly suspicious of how pharmaceutical companies influence the drugs they are prescribed.

Educated Consumers

Besides, they say, they have grown up watching their psychiatrists mix and match drugs in a manner that sometimes seems arbitrary, and they feel an obligation to supervise. "I tried Zoloft because my doctor said, 'I've had a lot of success with Zoloft,' no other reason," said Laurie, 26, who says researching medications to treat her depressive disorder has become something of a compulsion. "It's insane. I feel like you have to be informed because you're controlling your brain."

When a new psychiatrist suggested Seroquel, Laurie, who works in film production and who did not want her last name used, refused it because it can lead to weight gain. When the doctor suggested Wellbutrin XL, she replied with a line from the commercial she had seen dozens of times on television: "It has a low risk of sexual side effects. I like that."

But before agreeing to take the drug, Laurie consulted several Internet sites and the latest edition of the *Physicians' Desk Reference* guide to prescription drugs at the Barnes & Noble bookstore in Union Square. On a page of her notebook, she copied down the generic and brand names of seven alternatives. Effexor, she noted, helps with anxiety—a plus. But Wellbutrin suppresses appetite—even better. At the weekly meetings of an "under-30" mood-disorder support group in New York that Laurie attends, the discussion inevitably turns to medication. Group members trade notes on side effects that, they complain, doctors often fail to inform them about. Some say they are increasingly suspicious of how pharmaceutical companies influence the drugs they are prescribed.

"Lamictal is the new rage," said one man who attended the group, "but in part that's because there's a big money interest in it. You have to do research on your own because the research provided to you is not based on an objective source of what may be best."

This view of psychology as a series of problems that can be solved with pills is relatively brand new.

Recent reports that widely prescribed antidepressants could be responsible for suicidal thoughts or behavior in some adolescents have underscored for Laurie and other young adults how little is known about the risks of some drugs, and why different people respond to them differently. Moreover, drugs widely billed as nonaddictive, like Paxil or Effexor, can cause withdrawal symptoms, which some patients say they only learned of from their friends or fellow sufferers.

"This view of psychology as a series of problems that can be solved with pills is relatively brand new," said Andrea Tone, a professor of the social history of medicine at McGill University. "It's more elastic, and more subjective, so it lends itself more to taking matters into our own hands."

To that end, it helps to have come of age with the Internet, which offers new possibilities for communication and commerce to those who want to supplement their knowledge or circumvent doctors.

Fluent in Psychopharmacology

People of all ages gather on public Internet forums to trade notes on "head meds," but participants say the conversations are dominated by a younger crowd for whom anonymous exchanges of highly personal information are second nature. On patient-generated sites like CrazyBoards, fluency in the language of psychopharmacology is taken for granted. Dozens of drugs are referred to in passing by both brand name and generic, and no one is reticent about suggesting medications and dosage levels. . . .

Still, for some young adults, consulting their peers leads to taking less medicine, not more. When Eric Wisch, 20, reported to an anonymous online group that he was having problems remembering things, several members suggested that he stop taking Risperdal, one of four medications in a cocktail that had been mixed different ways by different doctors. "I decided to cut back," said Mr. Wisch, a sophomore at the University of Rochester who runs www.thebipolarblog.com, where he posts his thoughts on medications and other subjects. "And I'm doing better." Despite frequent admonitions on all the sites to "check with your Pdoc," an abbreviation for psychiatrist, there are also plenty of tips on how to get medications without a prescription.

"I know I shouldn't order drugs online," one participant wrote in a Sept. 26 posting on the Psycho-babble discussion group. "But I've been suffering with insomnia and my Pdoc isn't keen on sleep aids." What should he do, the poster wanted to know, after an order he placed with an online pharmacy that promised to provide sleeping pills without a prescription failed to deliver? Another regular participant, known as "med-empowered," replied that the poster was out of luck, and went on to suggest a private e-mail exchange: "I think I know some sites where you could post your experience and also get info about more reliable sites."

Drugs Are Available on the Web

For a hefty markup, dozens of Web sites fill orders for drugs, no prescription required, though to do so is not legal. Instead, customers are asked to fill out a form describing themselves and their symptoms, often with all the right boxes helpfully pre-checked.

Erin, 26, a slender hair stylist, remembers laughing to herself as she listed her weight as 250 pounds to order Adipex, a diet pill, for $113. One recent night, she took an Adipex to stay up cleaning her house, followed by a Xanax when she needed to sleep. Like many other self-medicators, Erin, who has been on and off antidepressants and sleeping pills since she was in high school, has considered weaning herself from the pills. She wishes she had opted for chamomile tea instead of the Xanax when she wanted to sleep. "I feel like I have been so programmed to think, 'If I feel like this then I should take this pill,'" she said. "I hate that." . . .

Online pharmacies are not the only way for determined self-prescribers to get their pills. Suffering from mood swings a decade after his illness was diagnosed as bipolar disorder,

Rich R., 31, heard in an online discussion group about an antidepressant not available in the United States. A contractor in the Midwest, Rich scanned an old prescription into his computer, rearranged the information and faxed it to pharmacies in Canada to get the drug. "My initial experience with physicians who are supposed to be experts in the field was disappointing," Rich said. "So I concluded I can do things better than they can."

Even for psychiatrists, patients say, the practice of prescribing psychotropic drugs is often hit and miss. New drugs for depression, anxiety and other problems proliferate. Stimulants like Adderall are frequently prescribed "as needed." Research has found that antidepressants affect different patients differently, so many try several drugs before finding one that helps. And in many cases, getting doctors to prescribe antidepressants, sleeping pills or other psychiatric medications is far from difficult, patients say.

The result is a surplus of half-empty pill bottles that provides a storehouse for those who wish to play pharmacist for their friends. The rules of the CrazyBoards Web site prohibit participants from openly offering or soliciting pharmaceuticals. But it is standard practice for people who visit the site to complain, tongue-in-cheek, that they simply "don't know what to do" with their leftovers. The rest takes place by private e-mail. Sometimes, the person requesting the drugs already has a prescription, but because the medications are so expensive, receiving them free from other people has its merits.

A Post-hurricane Care Package

Dan Todd, marooned in Covington, La., after Hurricane Katrina, said he would be forever grateful to a woman in New Hampshire who organized a donation drive for him among the site's regular participants. Within two days of posting a message saying that he had run out of his medications, he received several care packages of assorted mood stabilizers and anti-anxiety drugs, including Wellbutrin, Klonopin, Trileptal, Cymbalta and Neurontin. . . .

It doesn't always work out so well. When Katherine took a Xanax to ease her anxiety before a gynecologist appointment, she found that she could not keep her eyes open. She had traded a friend for the blue oval pill and she had no idea what the dosage was.

An Adderall given to her by another friend, she said, "did weird things to me." And Mr. Tylutki, who took the Ritalin she offered one weekend, began a downward spiral soon after. "I completely regretted and felt really guilty about it," Katherine said.

Taking Katherine's pills with him when he returned to Minneapolis, Mr. Tylutki took several a day while pursuing a nursing degree and working full time. Like many other students, he found Ritalin a useful study aid. One night, he read a book, lay down to sleep, wrote the paper in his head, got up, wrote it down, and received an A-minus. But he also began using cocaine and drinking too much alcohol. A few months ago, Mr. Tylutki took a break from school. He flushed the Ritalin down the toilet and stopped taking all drugs, including the Prozac that he had asked a doctor for when he began feeling down.

"I kind of made it seem like I needed it," Mr. Tylutki said, referring to what he told the doctor. "Now I think I was just lacking sleep."

Teens Use Prescription Drugs to Get High

Donna Leinwand

Donna Leinwand is a staff writer for USA Today.

When a teenager in Jan Sigerson's office mentioned a "pharm party" in February [2006], Sigerson thought the youth was talking about a keg party out on a farm.

"Pharm," it turned out, was short for pharmaceuticals, such as the powerful painkillers Vicodin and OxyContin. Sigerson, program director for Journeys, a teen drug treatment program in Omaha, soon learned that area youths were organizing parties to down fistfuls of prescription drugs. Since [that] February, several more youths at Journeys have mentioned that they attended pharm parties, Sigerson says. "When you start to see a pattern, you know it's becoming pretty widespread," she says. "I expect it to get worse before it gets better."

Drug counselors across the USA are beginning to hear about similar pill-popping parties, which are part of a rapidly developing underground culture that surrounds the rising abuse of prescription drugs by teens and young adults. It's a culture with its own lingo: Bowls and baggies of random pills often are called "trail mix," and on Internet chat sites, collecting pills from the family medicine chest is called "pharming."

Prescription pills have become popular among youths because they are easy to get and represent a more socially acceptable way of getting high than taking street drugs.

Carol Falkowski, director of research communications for the Hazelden Foundation, says young abusers of prescription drugs also have begun using the Internet to share "recipes" for getting high. Some websites are so simplistic, she says, that they refer to pills by color, rather than their brand names, content or potency. That, Falkowski says, could help explain why emergency rooms are reporting that teens and young adults increasingly are showing up overdosed on bizarre and potentially lethal combinations of pills.

Overdoses of prescription and over-the-counter drugs accounted for about one-quarter of the 1.3 million drug-related emergency room admissions in 2004, the federal Substance Abuse and Mental Health Services Administration reported [in May 2006].

The abuse of prescription and over-the-counter drugs— which barely registered a blip in drug-use surveys a decade ago [in the late nineties]—is escalating at what Falkowski and other analysts say is an alarming rate. In a 2005 survey by the Partnership for a Drug-Free America, 19% of U.S. teenagers— roughly 4.5 million youths—reported having taken prescription painkillers such as Vicodin or OxyContin or stimulants such as Ritalin or Adderall to get high.

Prescription drugs are familiar mood-altering substances for a generation that grew up as prescriptions soared for Ritalin and other stimulants to treat maladies such as attention-deficit disorder

---

Vicodin has been particularly popular in recent years; a study by the University of Michigan in 2005 found that nearly 10% of 12th-graders had used it in the previous year. About 5.5% said they had used OxyContin. Both drugs are now more popular among high school seniors than Ecstasy and cocaine. Marijuana is still the most popular drug by far; about one-third of the 12th-graders surveyed said they had used it in the previous year.

More Socially Acceptable

Falkowski, whose foundation is a treatment center based in Center City, Minn., says prescription pills have become popular among youths because they are easy to get and represent a more socially acceptable way of getting high than taking street drugs. Some kids, she says, are self-medicating undiagnosed depression or anxiety, while others are using stimulants to try to get an edge on tests and studying.

Falkowski says prescription drugs are familiar mood-altering substances for a generation that grew up as prescriptions soared for Ritalin and other stimulants to treat maladies such as attention-deficit disorder. "Five million kids take prescription drugs every day for behavior disorders," she says. "It's not unusual for kids to share pills with their friends. There have been incidents where kids bring a Ziploc baggie full of pills to school and share them with other kids." Pharm parties, she says, are "simply everyone pooling whatever pills they have together and having a good time on a Saturday night. Kids . . . don't think about the consequences."

Police, teachers and parents are so fixated on street drugs such as marijuana, cocaine and Ecstasy that they are missing the start of an epidemic.

Lisa Cappiello, 39, of Brooklyn, N.Y., says that seemed to be the case with her son, Eddie. She says she knew that he had tried marijuana at 15 and sneaked beers at school. But it wasn't until after he graduated from high school and took a year off before college that Cappiello realized the extent of her son's drug use—and the hold prescription drugs had on him. "In what seemed like the blink of an eye, it went from marijuana and an occasional beer to so much Xanax that (one day) my husband had to pick him up when he fell asleep on a street corner waiting for some friends," she said. "He hid his drug use from me so well."

The next day, Eddie Cappiello admitted to his parents that he had taken 15 pills of Xanax, a brand name for benzodiazepine that acts as a sedative. He told his parents Xanax helped him deal with anxiety and depression. Eddie rejected professional help and vowed to stop taking pills, his mother says. He was clean for 10 months, she says, before he was hospitalized in July 2005 after overdosing. Two months later, he entered a 28-day treatment program, his mother says. After he was discharged, he stayed clean for about two months—then relapsed into weekend binging: 40 to 50 pills and a quart of Jack Daniel's, sometimes by himself, sometimes with friends, Lisa Cappiello says.

Eddie Cappiello, 22, died in his bed on Feb. 17 after overdosing on a mix of pharmaceuticals. He left behind a girlfriend and two young children. A toxicology report said he had 134 milligrams of Xanax—the equivalent of 67 pills—and an opioid derivative in his system, his mother says.

"Before four years ago, I never even heard the word Xanax," Lisa Cappiello says. "Now . . . I know kids as young as 12 are using it. Then I found out that Vicodin was a very big party drug. Before school, after school, at parties. Kids mixed them with alcohol and Ecstasy. It was baffling to me."

Cappiello says police, teachers and parents are so fixated on street drugs such as marijuana, cocaine and Ecstasy that they are missing the start of an epidemic. "Eddie was not the first kid to die in this neighborhood from prescription drugs," she says.

'Troubling Trend'

In recent months, federal anti-drug officials have acknowledged that they didn't anticipate the quick escalation of prescription-drug abuse. Most government-sponsored drug prevention programs focus on marijuana, tobacco, alcohol and methamphetamine.

"We were taken by surprise when we started to see a high instance of abuse of prescription drugs," says Nora Volkow, director of the National Institute of Drug Abuse (NIDA), which is collecting information about how teens perceive, get and use prescription drugs so it can try to craft an effective prevention campaign. In a bulletin [in 2005], NIDA called the increase in pharmaceutical drug abuse among teens "disturbing" and said pharm parties were a "troubling trend."

The increasing availability of prescription drugs is a big reason for the rise in their abuse, Volkow and other drug specialists say. Pharmaceutical companies' production of two often-abused prescription drugs—hydrocodone and oxycodone, the active ingredients in drugs such as Vicodin and OxyContin—has risen dramatically as the drugs' popularity for legitimate uses has increased. Drug companies made 29 million doses of oxycodone in 2004, up from 15 million four years earlier. Hydrocodone doses rose from 14 million in 2000 to 24 million in 2004.

The 2005 Partnership survey found that more than three in five teens can easily get prescription painkillers from their parents' medicine cabinets. And as Falkowski says, the rising number of youths being treated with stimulants has made it easier for kids to use such drugs illicitly. About 3% of children are treated with a stimulant such as Adderall or Ritalin, up from less than 1% in 1987.

Almost all of the 13 youths at Phoenix House's intensive outpatient treatment program on New York City's Upper West Side have dabbled in prescription drugs, director Tessa Vining says. "There's definitely easy access," she says. "Maybe a parent had some surgery and took one or two painkillers from a bottle of 10, and the rest are just hanging out in the medicine cabinet."

After her son died, Cappiello says she wondered how kids in her area were getting pills. She says she learned from police that one local dealer got Xanax from his mother, who had been given a prescription for the drug. Instead of taking the pills, she gave them to her son to sell for $2 to $3 each.

Paul Michaud, 18, of Boston, says he got his first taste of OxyContin pills—he calls them OCs—from a friend during his freshman year in high school. Until then, Michaud says, he had smoked marijuana daily and taken a Percocet pill occasionally. Michaud's father had recently died of cancer, and Michaud says he was depressed and feeling like an outsider at school. The prescription painkiller made him feel like nothing could faze him, he recalls.

"The first time I did it, I was hooked," says Michaud, who is four months into a yearlong drug treatment program at Phoenix House in Springfield, Mass. He says he quickly became a daily OxyContin user, breaking apart the time-release capsules, crushing pills and snorting the powder from five 80-milligram pills a day. "They're not very hard to get. I could find OCs easier than I could find pot," Michaud says. "There were plenty of people who sold them," including some dealers who got pills illicitly by mail order.

Cutting Off the Supply

To try to reduce the supply of prescription drugs on the black market, authorities have shut down several "pill mills"—where doctors prescribe inordinate amounts of narcotics—as well as Internet pharmacies that ship drugs with little medical consultation, says Catherine Harnett, chief of demand reduction for the Drug Enforcement Administration (DEA). [In] September [2005], DEA agents arrested 18 people allegedly responsible for 4,600 such pharmacies.

Kids have been lulled into believing that good medicine can be used recreationally.

A tricky part of the prescription-drug problem, Harnett says, is addressing the perception among youths that pills are safe because they are "medicine." Many teens don't equate taking such pills with using drugs such as heroin or cocaine, she says.

"If you start with pills, it seems fairly sanitary and legitimate," she says. "Kids have been lulled into believing that good medicine can be used recreationally." Two in five teens in the Partnership study said prescription medicines, even if they are not prescribed by a doctor, are "much safer" to use than illegal drugs.

A Lot to Live For

Phil Bauer of York, Pa., believes his son, Mark, 18, an avid weight lifter, started using prescription drugs to relieve chronic back pain and didn't appreciate the potential risks of taking the drugs. Bauer says his son never behaved as he imagined a drug addict would. "He wasn't hanging out all night. He had parents who wouldn't let him do that."

Mark Bauer died of an overdose on May 28, 2004. The toxicology report found morphine, oxycodone and acetaminophen—the active ingredient in Tylenol but also an ingredient in Vicodin—in his system, Phil Bauer says. Before his son's death, "we didn't see a bleary-eyed guy. He wasn't slurring his words," the father says. "He seemed to have a lot to live for. I did not know prescription-drug abuse was a problem. There's so much guilt in that. I don't know if I stuck my head in the ground. I did not see this coming."

Michaud says he didn't equate his OxyContin addiction with hard-core drug abuse. "Where I come from, OC is a rich boys' drug," he says. "I thought, heroin abuse, that's pretty low. I'd never stick a needle in my arm." However, Michaud says he eventually switched to heroin. "I sniffed it and a week later, I was shooting," he says. "I thought I wasn't like other people doing heroin. I wasn't that low. Come to figure out, it all leads to the same place."

Organizations to Contact

The editors have compiled the following list of organizations concerned with the issues debated in this book. The descriptions are derived from materials provided by the organizations. All have publications or information available for interested readers. The list was compiled on the date of publication of the present volume; the information provided here may change. Readers need to remember that many organizations take several weeks or longer to respond to inquiries.

Alliance for the Prudent Use of Antibiotics (APUA)
5 Kneeland St., Boston, MA   02111
(617) 636-0966 • fax: (617) 636-3999
e-mail: apua@tufts.edu
Web site: www.tufts.edu/med/apua

APUA's mission is to strengthen society's defenses against infectious disease by promoting appropriate antimicrobial access and use and by controlling antimicrobial resistance on a worldwide basis. Its Web site offers extensive information for consumers and doctors about the proper use of antibiotics and the danger that overuse will lead to their ineffectiveness.

Center for Public Integrity
910 Seventeenth St., NW, 7th Fl., Washington, DC   20006
(202) 466-1300
Web site: www.publicintegrity.org

The Center for Public Integrity is a nonprofit, nonpartisan, nonadvocacy, independent journalism organization. Its mission is to produce original investigative journalism about significant public issues to make institutional power more transparent and accountable. It conducts a project titled Pushing Prescriptions: How the Drug Industry Sells Its Agenda at Your Expense, which has a Web page on the organization's Web site with extensive information about the political influence of the pharmaceutical industry.

Children and Adults Against Drugging America (CHAADA)
e-mail: info@chaada.org
Web site: www.chaada.org

CHAADA is a membership organization whose goal is to raise awareness about the overmedicating of America and the deception occurring within the psychiatric profession—which it views as preying on innocent people, especially children, in order to turn a profit—and the dangers of the drugs used to treat alleged mental illnesses. CHAADA is against the use of all psychotropic drugs. Its Web site contains extensive material about personal experiences with adverse drug effects and about drug-related legislation.

Drug Policy Alliance (DPA)
70 W. Thiry-sixth St., 16th Fl., New York, NY   10018
(212) 613-8020 • fax: (212) 613-8021
Web site: www.drugpolicy.org

DPA is a politically active organization of people who believe that the nation's present drug policy does more harm than good. Although most of its material deals with illegal drugs, its Web site contains many articles on prescription drug abuse and on problems related to federal drug control.

Free Medicine Foundation
(573) 996-3333
Web site: www.freemedicinefoundation.com

The Free Medicine Foundation is a nationwide patient-advocacy organization that links patients to free or very low-cost prescription plans available to eliminate or substantially reduce their prescription costs. Its Web site contains information about how the program works as well as comments from patients.

Healthy Skepticism
34 Methodist St., Willunga, SA   5172
   Australia
Web site: www.healthyskepticism.org

Healthy Skepticism is an international nonprofit organization for health professionals and everyone with an interest in improving health. Its main aim is to improve health by reducing harm from misleading drug promotion. Its Web site has an extensive library of references dealing with pharmaceutical advertising and the effects it has on patterns of prescribing and medication usage. The organization also publishes *Healthy Skepticism International News.*

Institute for Safe Medication Practices (ISMP)
1800 Byberry Rd., Ste. 810, Huntingdon Valley, PA   19006
(215) 947-7797 • fax: (215) 914-1492
Web site: www.ismp.org

The ISMP is the nation's only nonprofit organization devoted entirely to medication error prevention and safe medication use. Its mission is to advance patient safety worldwide by empowering the health-care community, including consumers, to prevent medication errors. It publishes regular newsletters, including *ISMP Medication Safety Alert!* and *Safe Medicine,* available at its Web site, and offers a medication error reporting program.

International Coalition for Drug Awareness
Web site: www.drugawareness.org

This organization is a private, nonprofit group of physicians, researchers, journalists, and concerned citizens focused on "the world's most pervasive and subtle drug problem—prescription drugs." Its Web site has the full-length film *Prescription for Disaster,* an in-depth investigation into the symbiotic relationships between the pharmaceutical industry, the FDA, lobbyists, lawmakers, medical schools, and researchers. It also has material about individuals' bad experiences with prescription drugs and links to many sites about specific drug dangers.

International Federation of Pharmaceutical Manufacturers and Associations (IFPMA)

15 Ch. Louis-Dunant, PO Box 195, Geneva 20 1211
  Switzerland
e-mail: admin@ifpma.org
Web site: www.ifpma.org

IFPMA is a nonprofit, nongovernmental organization representing pharmaceutical industry associations from both developed and developing countries. It aims to encourage a global policy environment that is conducive to innovation in medicine, both therapeutic and preventative, for the benefit of patients around the world. Its Web site contains information about its position on issues such as improving access to health care, the ethical promotion of drugs, and the problem of counterfeit medicines.

National Council on Patient Information and Education (NCPIE)

4915 Saint Elmo Ave., Ste. 505, Bethesda, MD 20814
(301) 656-8565 • fax: (301) 656-4464
e-mail: ncpie@ncpie.info
Web site: www.talkaboutrx.org

NCPIE is a coalition of more than 125 diverse organizations whose mission is to stimulate and improve communication of information on appropriate medicine use to consumers and health-care professionals. NCPIE publishes educational resources, including *Make Notes & Take Notes to Avoid Medication Errors*. Its Web site contains a section designed to help caregivers and patients become well-informed medicine users who know where to go for reliable information and what questions to ask.

No Free Lunch

e-mail: contact@nofreelunch.org
Web site: www.nofreelunch.org

No Free Lunch is a nonprofit organization of health-care providers and medical students who believe that pharmaceutical promotion should not guide clinical practice. Its Web site has slide presentations on the relationship between physicians and the pharmaceutical industry as well as information for patients, including a directory of doctors who have pledged not to accept gifts from drug companies.

Partnership for Prescription Assistance
(888) 477-1669
Web Site: www.pparx.org

The Partnership for Prescription Assistance brings together America's pharmaceutical companies, doctors, other health-care providers, patient advocacy organizations, and community groups to help qualifying patients who lack prescription coverage get the medicines they need through the public or private program that is right for them. Its Web site contains information about the available programs for patients, caregivers, and doctors, plus patient testimonials.

Partnership for Safe Medicines
8100 Boone Blvd., Ste. 220, Vienna, VA   22182
www.safemedicines.org

Partnership for Safe Medicines is a group of organizations and individuals that have policies, procedures, or programs to protect consumers from counterfeit or contraband medicines. Its Web site includes a guide explaining how to avoid, deter, and report suspected counterfeit drugs, as well as a blog about the growing problem of drug counterfeiting.

Pharmaceutical Research and Manufacturers of America (PhRMA)
950 F St. NW, Washington, DC   20004
(202) 835-3400 • fax:(202) 835-3414
Web site: www.phrma.org

PhRMA represents the country's leading pharmaceutical research and biotechnology companies. Its mission is to conduct effective advocacy for public policies that encourage discovery of important new medicines. Its Web site contains newsletters, policy statements, fact sheets, and press releases.

PharmedOut
Georgetown University Dept. of Physiology and Biophysics
Box 571460, Washington, DC 20057
(202) 687-1191 • fax: (202) 687-7407
Web Site: www.pharmedout.org

PharmedOut is an independent, publicly funded project that empowers physicians to identify and counter inappropriate pharmaceutical promotion practices. Its Web site offers many links to YouTube videos, articles, and Web resources that are of interest to consumers as well as doctors.

United States Food and Drug Administration Center for Drug Evaluation and Research (CDER)
5600 Fishers La., HFD-240, Rockville, MD 20857
(888) 463-6332
e-mail: druginfo@fda.hhs.gov
Web site: www.fda.gov/cder

CDER is the U.S. government agency responsible for the testing of drugs. Its Web site offers detailed information about its policies and about specific drugs, including their official consumer information sheets. It also publishes the *FDA Drug Safety Newsletter.*

United States Pharmacopeia (USP)
12601 Twinbrook Pkwy., Rockville, Maryland 20852
(800) 227-8772
Web site: www.usp.org

The USP is an independent, science-based nonprofit public health organization. It is the official public standards-setting authority for all prescription and over-the-counter medicines, dietary supplements, and other health-care products manufactured and sold in the United States. Most of the material at its Web site is intended for medical professionals and requires payment for access.

White House Office of National Drug Control Policy (ONDCP)
Drug Policy Information Clearinghouse, PO Box 6000
Rockville, MD   20849
(800) 666-3332 • fax: (301) 519-5212
Web site: www.whitehousedrugpolicy.gov

The principal purpose of ONDCP is to establish policies, priorities, and objectives for the nation's drug control program. The goals of the program are to reduce illicit drug use, manufacturing, and trafficking, drug-related crime and violence, and drug-related health consequences. Although it is concerned mainly with illegal drugs, its Web site has a section on prescription drug abuse.

Worst Pills, Best Pills
Public Citizen, 1600 Twentieth St. NW
Washington, DC   20009
Web site: www.worstpills.org

The Web site Worst pills, Best Pills is researched, written, and maintained by Public Citizen's Health Research Group, a division of Public Citizen, which is a nonprofit, nonpartisan public interest group that represents consumer interests in Congress, the executive branch, and the courts. Although most of its information about specific drugs is accessible only to subscribers, its Web site contains a number of free consumer guides, including "Misprescribing and Overprescribing of Drugs," "Diseases Caused by Drugs," and "The Public Health Crisis of Adverse Drug Reactions," among others.

Bibliography

Books

John Abramson — *Overdosed America: The Broken Promise of American Medicine.* New York: HarperPerennial, 2005.

Marcia Angell — *The Truth About the Drug Companies: How They Deceive Us and What to Do About It.* New York: Random House, 2005.

Jerry Avorn — *Powerful Medicines: The Benefits, Risks, and Costs of Prescription Drugs.* New York: Knopf, 2004.

Samuel H. Barondes — *Better than Prozac: Creating the Next Generation of Psychiatric Drugs.* New York: Oxford University Press, 2005.

Jörg Blech — *Inventing Disease and Pushing Pills: Pharmaceutical Companies and the Medicalisation of Normal Life.* New York: Routledge, 2006.

Peter Breggin — *Medication Madness: True Stories of Mayhem, Murder, and Suicide Caused by Psychiatric Drugs.* New York: St. Martin's, 2008.

Howard Brody — *Hooked: Ethics, the Medical Profession, and the Pharmaceutical Industry.* Lanham, MD: Rowman and Littlefield, 2007.

Shannon Brownlee	*Overtreated: Why Too Much Medicine Is Making Us Sicker and Poorer.* New York: Bloomsbury, 2007.
Abigail Caplovitz	*Turning Medicine into Snake Oil: How Pharmaceutical Marketers Put Patients at Risk.* Trenton: New Jersey Public Interest Research Group Law and Policy Center, 2006. Available for download at http://njpirg.org.
Jay S. Cohen	*Overdose: The Case Against the Drug Companies.* New York: Tarcher/Penguin, 2004.
Peter Conrad	*The Medicalization of Society: On the Transformation of Human Conditions into Treatable Disorders.* Baltimore: Johns Hopkins University Press, 2007.
Greg Critser	*Generation Rx: How Prescription Drugs Are Altering American Lives, Minds, and Bodies.* Boston: Houghton Mifflin, 2005.
Richard DeGrandpre	*The Cult of Pharmacology: How America Became the World's Most Troubled Drug Culture.* Durham, NC: Duke University Press, 2006.
Richard A. Deyo and Donald L. Patrick	*Hope or Hype: The Obsession with Medical Advances and the High Cost of False Promises.* New York: AMACOM, 2005.

Katherine Eban — *Dangerous Doses: How Counterfeiters Are Contaminating America's Drug Supply.* New York: Harcourt, 2005.

Carl Elliott — *Better than Well: American Medicine Meets the American Dream.* New York: Norton, 2003.

Richard A. Epstein — *Overdose: How Excessive Government Regulation Stifles Pharmaceutical Innovation.* New Haven, CT: Yale University Press, 2006.

Jordan Goodman and Vivien Walsh — *The Story of Taxol: Nature and Politics in the Pursuit of an Anti-cancer Drug.* New York: Cambridge University Press, 2006.

Merrill Goozner — *The $800 Million Pill.* Berkeley and Los Angeles: University of California Press, 2004.

Katharine Greider — *The Big Fix: How the Pharmaceutical Industry Rips Off American Consumers.* New York: PublicAffairs, 2003.

Fran Hawthorne — *Inside the FDA: The Business and Politics Behind the Drugs We Take and the Food We Eat.* Hoboken, NJ: Wiley, 2005.

Fran Hawthorne — *The Merck Druggernaut: The Inside Story of a Pharmaceutical Giant.* Hoboken, NJ: Wiley, 2005.

David Healy   *Let Them Eat Prozac: The Unhealthy Relationship Between the Pharmaceutical Industry and Depression.* New York: New York University Press, 2004.

Jerome P. Kassirer   *On the Take: How Medicine's Complicity with Big Business Can Endanger Your Health.* New York: Oxford University Press, 2005.

Michael Kremer   *Strong Medicine: Creating Incentives for Pharmaceutical Research on Neglected Diseases.* Princeton, NJ: Princeton University Press, 2004.

Jacky Law   *Big Pharma: Exposing the Global Healthcare Agenda.* New York: Carroll & Graf, 2006.

Jie Jack Li   *Laughing Gas, Viagra, and Lipitor: The Human Stories Behind the Drugs We Use.* New York: Oxford University Press, 2006.

Barry Meier   *Pain Killer: A "Wonder" Drug's Trail of Addiction and Death.* Emmaus, PA: Rodale, 2003.

Ray Moynihan and Alan Cassels   *Selling Sickness: How the World's Biggest Pharmaceutical Companies Are Turning Us All into Patients.* New York: Nation Books, 2006.

David G. Nelson
The Cancer Treatment Revolution: How Smart Drugs and Other New Therapies Are Renewing Our Hope and Changing the Face of Medicine. Hoboken, NJ: Wiley, 2007.

Rick Ng
Drugs: From Discovery to Approval. Hoboken, NJ: Wiley-Liss, 2004.

Drew Pinsky
When Painkillers Become Dangerous: What Everyone Needs to Know About OxyContin and Other Prescription Drugs. Center City, MN: Hazelden, 2004.

Michael A. Santoro and Thomas M. Gorrie
Ethics and the Pharmaceutical Industry. New York: Cambridge University Press, 2005.

Timothy Scott
America Fooled: The Truth About Antidepressants, Antipsychotics, and How We've Been Deceived. Victoria, TX: Argo, 2006.

Robert L. Shook
Miracle Medicines: Seven Lifesaving Drugs and the People Who Created Them. New York: Portfolio, 2007.

Thomas Szasz
The Medicalization of Everyday Life: Selected Essays. Syracuse, NY: Syracuse University Press, 2007.

P. Roy Vagelos
Medicine, Science and Merck. New York: Cambridge University Press, 2004.

| Daniel Vasella | *Magic Cancer Bullet: How a Tiny Orange Pill Is Rewriting Medical History.* New York: HarperBusiness, 2003. |
| Robert Whitaker | *Mad in America: Bad Science, Bad Medicine, and the Enduring Mistreatment of the Mentally Ill.* Cambridge, MA: Perseus, 2003. |

Periodicals

Belinda Allan	"Pill Pushing," *Consumer*, March 2007.
Andrea Atkins	"The Latest and Greatest," *Woman's Day*, May 8, 2007.
Ronald Bailey	"Is Industry-Funded Science Killing You? The Overrated Risks and Underrated Benefits of Pharmaceutical Research 'Conflicts of Interest,'" *Reason*, October 2007.
Doug Bandow	"Demonizing Drugmakers: The Political Assault on the Pharmaceutical Industry," *Cato Policy Analysis*, May 8, 2003.
Barbara Basler	"Ties That Blind," *AARP Bulletin*, January/February 2008.
Carol Boyd et al.	"Adolescents' Motivations to Abuse Prescription Medications," *Pediatrics*, December 2006.
Robert Cohen	"Drug Firm Fraud May Cost Medicare Untold Billions," *Richmond* (VA) *Times-Dispatch*, February 22, 2007.

Lisa Davis et al. "The Best and Worst Drugs for Women," *Prevention*, March 2007.

Tasha Eichenseher "A Spoon Full of Sugar: What Drug Companies Don't Want You to Know," *E: The Environmental Magazine*, March 1, 2004.

Adriane Fugh-Berman "A Bone to Pick with Bone Drugs," *Women's Health Activist*, March 1, 2006.

Adriane Fugh-Berman "Unsafe IBS Drugs Back on the Market," *Women's Health Activist*, September 1, 2007.

Bill Gifford and Brian McClintock "Take Two and Cross Your Fingers," *Men's Health*, September 2006.

Brian Grow et al. "Bitter Pills," *Business Week*, December 18, 2006.

Jeneen Interlandi "The Anti-drug Drugs," *Newsweek* Web Exclusive, January 3, 2008. www.newsweek.com/id/83873.

Bruce Japsen "Suffering Boomers Want to Fill Vioxx Void: Celebrex Sales Surge Despite Possible Heart Risks; Firms Seek OK on New Pain Drugs," *Chicago Tribune*, March 23, 2007.

Joanne Kaufman "The Dangerous New High," *Reader's Digest*, November 2006.

Timothy F. Kim "Prescription Drug Abuse Problem Is Growing Rapidly in U.S., Especially Among Adolescents," *Pediatric News*, August 1, 2006.

Fred Kuhr   "The Next Line of Attack," *Advocate*, April 10, 2007.

Christopher Lane   "Shy on Drugs," *New York Times*, September 21, 2007.

Trudy Lieberman   "Bitter Pill: How the Press Helps Push Prescription Drugs, Sometimes with Deadly Consequences," *Columbia Journalism Review*, July 1, 2005.

Musa Mayer   "When Clinical Trials Are Compromised: A Perspective from a Patient Advocate," *PLoS Medicine*, November 2005.

Ray Moynihan and David Henry   "The Fight against Disease Mongering: Generating Knowledge for Action," *PLoS Medicine*, April 2006.

New York Times Upfront   "Prescription Drugs: Their Use and Abuse," February 20, 2006.

Carol Rados   "Orphan Products: Hope for People with Rare Diseases," *FDA Consumer*, November/December 2003.

Arnold S. Relman   "To Lose Trust, Every Day," *New Republic*, July 23, 2007.

Elizabeth Royte   "Drugging the Waters: How an Aging Population and Our Growing Addiction to Pharmaceuticals May Be Poisoning Our Rivers," *OnEarth*, Fall 2006.

Robert F. Service   "Orphan Drugs of the Future?" *Science*, March 19, 2004.

John Simons   "Blogging on Drugs," *Fortune*, June 11, 2007.

Miriam E. Tucker   "Prescription Drug Abuse Increases Among Teens," *Family Practice News*, October 1, 2007.

Wall Street Journal   "How About a 'Kianna's Law,'" March 24, 2005.

H. Gilbert Welch et al.   "What's Making Us Sick Is an Epidemic of Diagnoses," *New York Times*, January 2, 2007.

Kurt Williamsen   "Manipulating Medical Study Data: Studies on New Drugs and Medical Devices Are Being Manipulated by Their Manufacturers Through the Use of Flawed Studies, In-Pocket Experts, and Pressure on the FDA," *New American*, September 5, 2005.

Index

A

Redux (dexfenfluramine), 40, 42–44
Regulations
  advertising, 84, 94, 97–98, 103
  direct-to-consumer advertising, 103
  FDA lapses, 32–33
  FDA regulatory letters, 36, 101–102
  political will, 103–104
Reminder advertising, 85
Reuters Business Insights report, 90
Rezulin, 53
Risk-benefit analyis, 35, 66, 72–73, 77
RiskMAPS (risk management action plans), 69
Risperdal, 209
Ritalin, 105–106, 203, 212, 215
Rituxan, 151
Rofecoxib (Vioxx), 100
Rosuvastatin (Crestor), 30

S

SARS (severe acute respiratory syndrome), 175–176
Schweitzer, Albert, 158
Script tracking, 184–186
Searle, 24
Selective serotonin uptake inhibitors (SSRIs), 124–125
Self-medication, 64, 83, 204–205, 215
Selling Sickness (Moynihan), 96
SERM (selective estrogen receptor modulator), 71
Seroquel, 208
Severe acute respiratory syndrome (SARS), 175–176
Side effects, 19, 29–30, 38–39, 64, 190

60 Minutes (television), 198
Sleeping sickness (trypanosomiasis), 159–160
Sporanox (itraconazole), 98
SSRIs (selective serotonin uptake inhibitors), 124–125
Streptokinase, 59
Study of Tamoxifen and Raloxifene (STAR) trial, 73
Sulfanilamide, 50
Symptomatic treatment thresholds, 100–101

T

Tacrolimus (Protopic), 30
Tamoxifen, 71, 73
Tarceva, 150
Terbinafine (Lamisil), 85, 97–98
Terminally ill, 75–76
Thalidomide, 50, 163
Thebipolarblog.com, 209
Therapeutic categories, 121
Todd, Chris, 68
Trypanosomiasis (sleeping sickness), 159–160
Tufts Center for the Study of Drug Development, 128, 177
Tufts-New England Medical Center, 154
Tykerb, 150

U

Undiagnosed, untreated conditions, 127
U.S. General Accountability Office, 80, 124

V

Vaccines, 162
Vaniqa, 160
Vectibix, 155